# LAGOM

# LAGOM

## The Swedish Art of Balanced Living

**Linnea Dunne**

An Hachette UK Company
www.hachette.co.uk

First published in Great Britain in 2017 by Gaia, a division
of Octopus Publishing Group Ltd, Carmelite House,
50 Victoria Embankment, London EC4Y 0DZ
www.octopusbooks.co.uk

ISBN 978-1-85675-374-6

A CIP catalogue record for this book is available from the
British Library.

Printed and bound in Italy

10 9 8 7 6

Commissioning Editor: Leanne Bryan
Editor: Pollyanna Poulter
Copy Editor: Jo Richardson
Art Director: Yasia Williams
Illustrator: Naomi Wilkinson
Senior Production Manager: Katherine Hockley
Picture Research Manager: Giulia Hetherington

# CONTENTS

# Introduction

What is *lagom*, why should you care and if you do, how can you adopt it? From the Vikings to Zlatan and an unlikely *lagom* advocate, we bust some myths and prepare to "lagomify" our lives.

"Consensus is king and everyone mucks in."

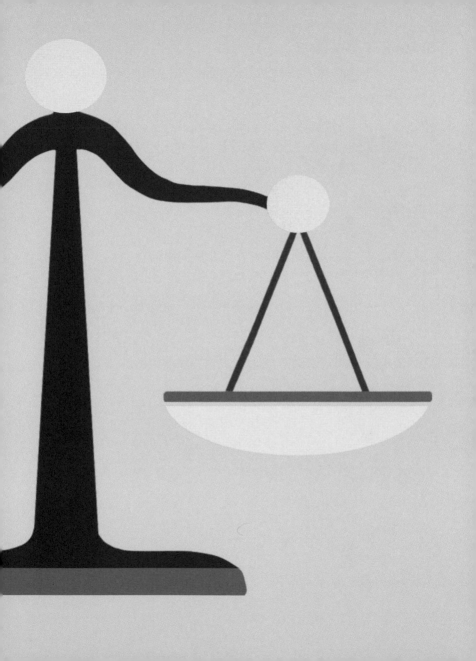

# WHAT IS LAGOM?
## – on Vikings, balance and semi-skimmed milk

**In 1996, Sweden got itself a new nickname. Author Jonas Gardell called it "the country of semi-skimmed milk", a moniker the Swedes took to heart and have been using ever since. In his standup show, the author described a country that celebrates balance and puts fairness on a pedestal, where consensus is king and everyone mucks in. He depicted a nation that loves white walls and functional design, and that deems semi-skimmed milk just perfect – not too skinny, not too fat. He characterized a country that is *lagom*.**

*Lagom* has no equivalent in the English language, but it loosely means "not too little, not too much, but just enough". It's widely believed that the word comes from the Viking term *laget om* – literally "around the team" – and derives from the custom of passing a horn of mead around and ensuring there was just enough for everyone to get a sip. But while the anecdote may hit the nail on the head, the true etymology of the word points to an old form of the word *lag*, a common sense type of "law".

### The law of *lagom*

So what's the law of *lagom*? At its simplest, the word describes something that's "just enough" or "just right" – like the right amount of milk in your coffee or the perfect pressure of a massage. Beyond the material world it becomes far more sophisticated, implying that the balancing act has reached perfection, and relying on a range of social codes. *Lagom* is accepting an invitation to spend the weekend at a friend's house, but bringing your own bed sheets because it's fair to share the burden of laundry. It's having the right to stay at home with a sick child – pay intact – but never abusing that right.

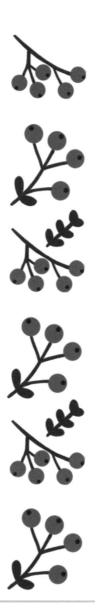

*Lagom* is buying a practical car – even if it's not the most visually pleasing of vehicles. It's painting just one feature wall in your lounge and leaving the rest white, because doing the entire room would be too much. It's wearing bright-red lipstick, but leaving the rest of your makeup perfectly understated. *Lagom* is having a burger but opting out of the fries, because moderation is a virtue; it's whipping up a brand-new dinner dish using nothing except leftovers, because waste is a mortal sin.

## Putting the law into practice

Postcard Sweden presents spacious rooms of minimalist décor sleek enough to promote a sense of calm in just one look. *Lagom* is a great deal about that space – about decluttering and simplifying, erasing prejudice and paving the way for honesty. In the bigger picture, the balance of *lagom* goes way beyond emotional wellbeing and interior design to become all about belonging and shared responsibility – not just fitting in, but being part of a greater entity. It's about relationships with your neighbours, looking after communal spaces and paying taxes that fund study groups (*see* page 122) and heavily subsidized culture schools (institutions for music and cultural tuition).

Recently described by the World Economic Forum as beating other countries at just about everything, Sweden has developed an enviable welfare state with generous parental packages and exceptionally low levels of corruption. In that regard, this country of semi-skimmed milk is the product of a skilful balancing act – protecting its people yet setting them free, together.

# MY RELATIONSHIP TO LAGOM
## – on the Law of Jante, busting some myths and a *lagom* approach to happiness

I was born and raised in Sweden, but left for Dublin aged 19, keen on adventure and to boost my worldliness. The contrast was dramatic, and I fell head over heels for Ireland's culture of spontaneous fun and never really caring about what's "just enough". With fellow Swedish ex-pats, I raved about a newfound freedom and the relief of not having to take things so seriously, only moments later to bemoan the failings of sorely lacking rental market regulation in Ireland and the madness of leaving heaps of garbage out in the street for collection.

You could say that I ran away from a life of *lagom*, or you could blame the Law of Jante. Penned by Danish–Norwegian author Aksel Sandemose in 1933 in an attempt to describe a certain attitude among fellow Scandinavians, the Law of Jante sets out ten rules that dictate the dos and don'ts of acceptable behaviour. Together, they depict a society that frowns upon individual success and achievement, a culture obsessed with rules. When *lagom* is occasionally criticized for being restrictive, it is linked to this – but is the criticism fair, and do the old rules even apply to 21st-century Sweden?

# A *lagom* kind of happiness

I'll admit that I was a little taken aback when I first heard about the idea of *lagom* as the new covetable approach to life, the Swedish secret to happiness. Admirable though its principles of balance are, were they in reality making Swedes exceptionally happy?

Now I can see the irony of the fact that I didn't immediately get it. Swedes may not be the happiest folk in the world, but they're consistently in the top ten of various happiness rankings. This is a *lagom* kind of happiness – not the elated or euphoric and definitely not the boastful kind, but measured. And it's exactly this quality of balance that would seem to be the secret to true, sustainable happiness. Just consult the psychology books (*see* pages 113–14).

## BUSTING SOME MYTHS

**MYTH:** *Lagom* **celebrates mediocrity.**

*Lagom* is unimpressed by individual achievement and surplus wealth because it's simply all about finding what works for the collective – and doing that well. But the results are far from mediocre. In fact, they've contributed to one of the most celebrated social welfare systems in the world.

**MYTH:** *Lagom* **is a thought-police state that enforces conformity.**

Swedes are highly opinionated and will happily engage in calm, rational debate for hours on end, to an extent that outsiders find infuriating. The end goal, however, is not the argument in itself, but the arrival at a decision everyone can get behind. That approach is not very tabloid but is hugely effective as far as a *lagom* society is concerned.

## MYTH: *Lagom* breeds stinginess.

Enter the old Swedish comic strip *Spara och Slösa*, roughly translating as "saving and wasting", aiming to teach children about the importance of saving money. The cartoon was commissioned in the 1920s by one of Sweden's main banks and should indeed be interpreted accordingly, yet I'll maintain that it does no such thing as celebrate stinginess. What it does is condemn waste. While excessive extravagance and mindless spending sprees are frowned upon, find a sophisticated new gadget that's been rigorously checked and awarded "best in test" and you'll soon see everyone jumping on the bandwagon, mutually approving each other's significant expenditure because it was a considered one.

## MYTH: *Lagom* frowns upon confidence and pride.

Manchester United forward Zlatan Ibrahimović is confidence and pride personified, and celebrated the world over as Sweden's big hero. In the words of Jonas Gardell (*see* page 8), always a central, flamboyant figure at Stockholm Pride, "A lot fits within the parameters for *lagom*. I'm quite an oddball, and even I fit in."

## WHY ADOPT IT?
— the benefits of *lagom*, from the inside and out

**DID YOU KNOW?**

According to happiness research, money makes us happy – but only to a degree. If we're poor, cash will add to our sense of happiness, but if we're already well off, more of it won't make us happier. A *lagom* amount of money is enough; beyond that, our happiness levels depend on other factors.

## "If you know what's 'just enough', why go overboard?"

You could say that *lagom* is a timely trend. With most people under stress, spending too much time staring at screens, feeling overloaded with toxins and regretting missing out on precious time with their kids and grannies, the planet is screaming out for an ethos of balance. Add to this that the natural resources are rapidly being depleted, and minimizing waste looks like a pretty urgent priority. If you know what's "just enough", why go overboard?

But the effects of *lagom* have, in fact, been making waves since long before the advent of global warming, social media and a 24/7 working world. Sometimes described as a family utopia, Sweden is a country with a large middle class and a strong welfare state. The huge majority of people enjoy a great quality of life, and there is balance in everything from free education to extensive recycling schemes. The mantra of aiming for "just enough" at all times comes with benefits for our inner psychological and emotional world as well as society at large. It's about affording our consciousness the space to just be and allowing enough latitude for change and development.

"With its loathing of waste and insistence on fairness, *lagom* is a crucial ingredient in Sweden's recipe for success."

## THE BENEFITS OF *LAGOM*

### #1: Physical space

Moderate, conscious consumption makes decluttering easier, and your home becomes a more peaceful place. With minimal Scandinavian design to boot, you may never want to leave the house.

### #2: Mental space

When you learn to take a step back and stop your mind spiralling, you can live life in a more authentic and focused way – embracing and coping with good and bad experiences, and being fully present both at work and at home.

### #3: Improved finances

As you become increasingly conscious not only of your personal needs but also those of the planet, you'll be likely to consume less while also learning to look after and be thrifty with your resources.

### #4: A sense of belonging

From improved relationships with your neighbours to trust in society's collective and shared responsibilities, a *lagom* attitude can help you feel part of something bigger and provide a sense of purpose.

# Key to a clarified life

You may be forgiven for thinking that *lagom* sounds exhausting, what with requiring a well-designed home, eating healthily, exercising, spending time with your friends, family and neighbours, achieving at work, being able to handle a spectrum of emotions yet feel contented most of the time and being constantly mindful of the environment while you're at it. But actually, *lagom* is all about making the good life less complicated.

The *lagom* approach of saying "stop" when you've had enough, but refusing to accept a sloppy solution for the sake of keeping things sweet means that getting things right is so much easier. And when we all muck in and deal with the really important stuff, everybody wins.

When I look at Sweden now, I don't see anyone sneering at ambition or shutting down debate. Instead I see huge numbers of people who care about getting things right; a place efficient enough to provide the space to breathe. With its loathing of waste and insistence on fairness, *lagom* is a crucial ingredient in Sweden's recipe for success. Be it through freedom from clutter and material obsession or liberation from unnecessary hours at your desk, *lagom* can elevate the meaning of quality of life – without stress, without squander, but with the clarity of an eccentric gay comedian who found a way to fit in with the country of semi-skimmed milk.

# Living lagom:
## work–life balance

Do the Swedes really have it all, and what's with all the male nannies? A look at Swedish work, equality and "me time" – and the best excuse ever to eat cinnamon buns.

# WORK–LIFE BALANCE
## – a snapshot of a *lagom* lifestyle

**DID YOU KNOW?**

Swedes have a near-religious relationship with their *fika* or coffee breaks. In traditional working environments, employees enjoy a 15-minute *fika* every morning and afternoon, in addition to their lunch break, often complete with home-baked pastries to go with the compulsory filter coffee.

Born of a culture with a Lutheran work ethic and strong unions, there's no denying that *lagom* takes work very seriously. Yet the importance of taking due time out of work is equally respected, with the majority of Swedish workers walking out the door the minute their contracted hours are up – and that's after a number of decent *fika* breaks (*see* left and page 36).

**TOP TIP**

According to sleep researcher Nathaniel Kleitman's work on the human ultradian rhythm, we are at our most effective if we allow the brain to unplug every 90 minutes. A University of Toronto study, meanwhile, found that the perfect formula for optimal productivity is to work for 52 minutes at a time followed by a 17-minute break. Find what works for you, and honour those breaks.

"If you do it right, you'll spend a *lagom* amount of time on it."

## Working outside the box

The *lagom* approach to work could be described simply as common sense, exemplified by the following scenario typical of the many reports I have had from the *lagom*-uninitiated (that is non-Swedish) in Swedish work contexts. The new recruit asks of her or his boss, "How long do you want me to spend on this task?" To which the invariable reply is: "Until it's ready." You'd think it goes without saying: don't waste time on a job that's already done well enough, but equally, don't deliver a job that's not up to scratch. If you do it right, you'll spend a *lagom* amount of time on it.

Perhaps a lack of anxiety around the definition of what a *lagom* amount of time actually is can be linked to the prevailing consensus culture and non-hierarchical company structures. Enter *förankringsprocessen*, a concept for running ideas by everyone impacted by them, allowing everyone to voice their opinion and then discussing everything in detail before arriving at a decision that everyone can get behind. And "everyone" doesn't just mean the board; it means the executives *and* the recently employed graduate, because who knows what groundbreaking perspective they might bring?

With this in mind, while it may seem surprising that Swedish businesses tend to rank as comparatively very efficient, you might begin to see why making a call on the completion of that task isn't so daunting. Similarly, you may be casually strolling out the door 20 minutes early, and that's also fine. Your colleagues, including your boss, will simply assume that your work is done; otherwise, you obviously wouldn't be leaving. A crucial theme is trust – something we'll return to later in the book.

**TOP TIP**

Leave work on time. Research has shown that it makes us both happier and more productive.

**DID YOU KNOW?**

The average Swede works 1,644 hours per year, compared with the OECD (Organisation for Economic Co-operation and Development) average of 1,776 hours. And yet Sweden ranks sixth in the global competitiveness index.

## Calling *lagom* time

The *lagom* work–life balance is supported in Sweden by its tradition of almost shutting down for the summer, with most professionals taking at least four consecutive weeks off for a proper summer break. In addition, parents get generous parental leave as well as the right to flexible working, or at least working shorter days, for the first eight years of a child's life.

But even without such recreational benefits, we can take the *lagom* lead and spend as many of our evenings as we can with family or friends, cooking and eating dinner and chatting about the events of the day. And when it comes to Friday, there is the Swedish example of *fredagsmys* (*see* page 24) to follow, the ultimate comfort eating experience featuring a pick-'n'-mix taco buffet, crisps and dips while vegging on the couch in front of the TV. What better way to kick off the weekend than in true *lagom* style?

# FREDAGSMYS
## – honouring downtime with loved ones

Combining that Friday feeling with a commitment to cosying up with your loved ones (*mys* is Swedish for "cosiness" – eat your heart out *hygge*), *fredagsmys* has become such a sacred concept in Swedish culture that there are well-known commercial jingles celebrating it. Cue an evening of crisps and tracksuit bottoms (or *mjukisbyxor*, literally meaning "soft trousers") that's all about switching off and putting your feet up.

### TOP TIP #1

Make it your primary aim to keep it simple. Swedes, who might otherwise be quite keen on the whole DIY thing in the kitchen, will happily buy store-bought dip mixes and taco kits with ready-made salsa on a Friday, all in the name of making it easy for themselves.

### TOP TIP #2

To put the *"mys"* into *fredagsmys*, make sure you always have plenty of candles, including tealights, at home, get your favourite loungewear out and light(en) up.

## What's *lagom* about it?

Well, for one, it balances out any notions about healthy eating and early bedtimes from school nights in favour of simply doing what feels good. In fact, *fredagsmys* works as an excuse for just about anything – as long as there isn't too much effort involved. No food is too basic or ready-made for *fredagsmys*, no TV show too mind-numbingly shallow. If you're comfortable and not worrying, then you're doing it right.

# TACOS, FREDAGSMYS STYLE
## – a step-by-step guide to a couch feast

Forget *pico de gallo*, *frijoles negros* and chipotle sauce. *Fredagsmys*-style tacos have little to do with authenticity and everything to do with simple, sociable eating. So here's the lowdown on how to create that laid-back yet pampering, uniquely *lagom* vibe.

### Get some bowls

If you have pretty little colourful bowls handy, those will add to the cheerful Friday feeling, but any will do – big or small, typically used for breakfast cereal, olives, soup or baby food. Swedish tacos take sociable self-service to the next level, so you'll want to adopt that pick-'n'-mix mindset.

### Choose your main filling

If you're a meat eater and a tad old school, opt for minced beef. Veggie? Think halloumi and roasted cubes of sweet potato or butternut squash. The only limit here is your imagination. Advanced *fredagsmys*-ers can make their own spice mix – just use your own preferred blend of smoked paprika, ground cumin, ground coriander, chilli powder and some salt and pepper, and finish with a touch of lime juice. Feeling exceptionally Friday lazy? No one will blame you for buying a ready-made taco kit!

### Chop some veg

Cucumber, lettuce, tomatoes and sweet peppers make nice additional fillings, and all you have to do is chop them and fill those bowls. A can of corn kernels works well, too.

### The finishing touches

Grate some cheese, open up a jar of salsa and get your choice of tortilla wraps or taco shells out of the cupboard. If you're feeling fancy, by all means make your own guacamole and salsa with lots of lime, fresh coriander and maybe some chopped chilli. You could pull out all the stops and add cubed feta cheese or pulled pork – but, crucially, if you're not that way inclined, just the basics will do.

### Enjoy!

Whether in front of the TV or at the kitchen table, don some cosy woolly socks, dim the room lights and let everyone dive in.

# EQUALITY AND FAMILY LIFE
## – on latte dads, subsidized childcare and an efficient economy

What's with all the male nannies? The question, posed by a foreign journalist, was snapped up and spread by Swedes with smug amusement so quickly that no one seems to know anymore where it came from, or indeed if it's just an urban myth. But no, Swedes aren't exceptionally likely to hire male nannies – nor are they likely to need nannies at all. But Swedish fathers are more likely to take paternity leave and be seen pushing a buggy with one hand and sipping coffee with the other. We call them *lattepappor*, "latte dads", after *lattemammor*, the equivalent of "yummy mummies".

### Founding a parents' utopia

**DID YOU KNOW?**

The percentage of working women in Sweden is the highest in the European Union, at 78.3%.

In 1974, Sweden became the first country in the world to replace gender-specific maternity leave with parental leave. It was initially introduced as a right to three months' paid time off work for each parent, with the father allowed to sign his days over to the mother if that worked for the couple. But it wasn't until the use-it-or-lose-it rule was brought in that real change happened – in 1995, a dedicated "daddy month" was established, and now three months are earmarked for each parent.

In total, Swedish parents are entitled to 480 days of parental leave when a child is born or adopted, to be taken by either parent at any time before the child turns eight. They also get paid time off work to care for a sick child (termed VAB, which stands for *vård av barn*, with the month of February now notoriously known as *Vabruari*). Add a highly subsidized and quality-controlled childcare system, with all children aged one or over guaranteed a place in kindergarten at an almost insignificant fraction

## HOW EQUAL IS YOUR RELATIONSHIP?

From childcare duties to household chores, sharing domestic tasks equally can contribute to both happier parents and happier kids.

## TOP TIP FOR FATHERS

If you're a dad without the right to paternity leave, there are other ways to step up to a more equal family life. Take on a bigger share of the days at home with sick kids once your partner is back at work, shoulder the lunchbox planning and make sure that your kids see you doing the laundry. *Lagom* is in the little things...

of the real cost, and you'll see why Sweden is often described as a utopia for parents.

## How equality relates to *lagom*

The most gender-equal countries also typically score higher than other countries on the happiness scale. Businesses that are more gender equal do better: their employees are happier, and they have a low turnover of staff, high retention rates, higher job satisfaction and higher productivity rates. Moreover, more egalitarian couples are happier – and that goes not just for both partners, but for any children they may have. Their kids do better in school, are less likely to need to see a psychiatrist or need medication. Mothers in equal relationships are healthier, happier and less depressed, and fathers are healthier, smoke less, drink less and are less likely to suffer from depression.

## Family-friendly benefits

The 2016 Happiness Index, collated by employee intelligence platform Butterfly, found a very strong correlation between work–life balance and overall employee happiness. Indeed, employees from across the globe confirmed that the area in which their employers were failing them the most was work–life balance, with a willingness to change systems, processes and conditions to improve workload and flexibility being key for employers to increase employee happiness levels.

Put simply, gender equality and family-friendly policies are beneficial on a personal level as well as with regard to both micro- and macro-economics. Everybody wins.

# "ME TIME"
## – creativity and the importance of downtime

So, you can't simply wave a wand to whip up a childcare system costing you no more than 1,287 SEK (approximately €135 or £112) per month for a full-time place in kindergarten? Work–life balance is about more than just the time you spend in work while your kids are in childcare – the importance of spare time is not to be overlooked.

As companies throughout Sweden started trialling a six-hour working day, one of the motivating factors was an awareness of the significant benefits of downtime and room for hobbies. Many employers realized that as a consequence they became a far more attractive prospect, resulting in more job applicants and happier and more effective employees.

**DID YOU KNOW?**

It's been proven that both creativity and time in nature contribute to increased happiness. Take up journalling, join a painting class or make a habit out of going for a lunchtime walk. The more regular the activity, the more you'll feel the benefit in terms of increased contentedness as well as productivity in work.

## Recharging our batteries

With a neuroscience hat on, it makes perfect sense. The parasympathetic nervous system (PSNS) is the part of our makeup that helps to calm us down and recharge after our sympathetic nervous system (SNS) has driven us to go, go, go. The SNS is characterized by short-term thinking, a sensitivity to threat and an intense drive. It can seem productive and efficient, but if uninterrupted it will push us into fight-or-flight mode and lead to exhaustion. A bit like an athlete doing sprint/recovery training, we need our PSNS, and downtime – whether it's football or knitting or playing the piano – is what it's all about. When we talk about recharging our batteries, this is it; it's *lagom* because it cuts you some slack right now, but you'll also reap the benefits many times over in the long term.

# Creative use of time

Considering their serious approach to work and education, Swedes do spare time pretty well. Associations and group activities are big in Sweden, and many children learn an instrument or similar at culture school (*see* page 9). After-school child care is called *fritids* – literally "free time" – which says a thing or two about the shared view of what time after school should be all about. The result is a nation that doesn't just do well in business, but exceptionally so in the creative fields. Stockholm alone boasts almost as many tech startups as Silicon Valley; and on the music side, Sweden is the world's largest exporter of chart music per capita.

Finding the space for "me time" might seem hard if your employer isn't all that into the idea of a six-hour working day, but it doesn't take much – and what it costs in time, you often get back many times over in increased focus and a boost in energy. If you gave up one TV show, which might be fleetingly enjoyable but is unlikely to be rewarding in the long term, and a social media session a day, you might free up five minutes every evening for journalling or one evening a week for an evening class – you'll be surprised by how much the creative juices start flowing.

# INTRODUCING FIKA
## – because it's good for business and everybody loves free cinnamon buns

Few things aid the honouring of regular breaks and downtime like *fika*, the coffee break elevated to new heights by the Swedes. While *fika* is a constant in all parts of Swedish society, its importance in the working world cannot be overstated.

### More than just a coffee break

Fika is an institution in itself, which we'll return to in the next chapter (*see* page 40), but in the context of work, it serves a number of very *lagom* functions. If there's a practice in place that makes a proper 10am break acceptable, surely that can only be a good thing? If, in addition, it means that people don't just take their eyes off their screen for 15 minutes or more but also end up chatting to each other, catching up about industry news or the challenges of the afternoon's client pitch, it can take both the office culture and the company output to the next level. Note the differences between *fika* and elevenses. More than just topping up your coffee, *fika* is about an exchange, a connection; about unplugging from the task at hand and being present with your colleagues in true *lagom* style.

### The *fika* startup

Getting your workplace to adopt a proper *fika* culture might be a challenge, but start small and you'll be able to reap many of the benefits. Ask your desk neighbour along for your morning trip to the kitchen or coffee machine, or offer to make them tea. The next time you need a face-to-face chat with a colleague, suggest meeting in the staff room or canteen. If you feel ambitious, volunteer to get a Friday *fika* routine happening. I can't see too many people kicking up a storm over being fed cinnamon buns before heading home for *fredagsmys* (*see* page 24).

# Eating lagom:
## food, drink & fika

Learn to cook, forage and grow your own veg
like a Swede. From picnics and moderate eating
to New Nordic Cuisine, here's everything
you need to know about eating *lagom*.

2

# FIKA
## – life's silver lining

Swedes are in the top three of the biggest coffee consumers in the world, a habit closely linked to *fika* culture. I spent hours on end most afternoons in upper secondary school in my favourite café chatting to friends, and I hold those memories very dear. There was nothing particularly *lagom* about the endless free top-ups of tar-like black filter coffee I consumed on a daily basis back then, but put it into context and the institution of *fika* certainly adds to the balance of Swedish culinary tradition.

**DID YOU KNOW?**

In 2012, the average Swede consumed 7.32kg (16lb) of coffee, compared with the 4.83kg (10²/₃lb) average for the European Union.

### *Fika lagom*-style

In a culture otherwise keen on balanced meals and healthy eating, *fika* adds a silver lining. On an ordinary Wednesday, just a cookie might do, but frequently the tradition calls for pulling out all the stops. As part of a playdate, a *fika* may include open sandwiches and fruit before the cinnamon buns come out, but a typical weekend *fika* is all about the goodies: think a table full of cakes and cookies, complete with pretty coffee cups and candles. And still: Swedes do indulge, but not too much. Which means you might help yourself to one of each type of cookie, but not two cakes – and never ever the last one of anything. It takes a child or a non-Swede to empty all the plates during a typical *fika* session, otherwise the last cookie will always stay put.

*Fika* is to Swedes what pubs are to the Brits and *aperitivo* is to Italians: a break from doing. At a time of constant social media notifications and 24/7 work emails, *fika* can be a way to pause, relax and connect – with yourself, your loved ones, colleagues or a book. Leave out the endless top-ups, and *fika* will seem very *lagom* indeed compared with a night of pints or wine and free olives.

# KANELBULLAR
## – cinnamon buns

No one pastry or baked treat says *fika* time as much as a cinnamon-flavoured bun, paired here with a touch of aromatic cardamom. Think of that gorgeous warmly spicy scent spreading throughout your home while the buns are baking in the oven, and you'll soon understand why Swedes have an almost sacred relationship with cinnamon.

**Makes:** 10 buns

sunflower oil, for oiling

300ml (10fl oz/½ pint) milk

1 teaspoon ground cardamom

50g (1¾oz) butter

425g (15oz) plain flour,
plus extra for dusting

7g (¹/₃oz) packet fast-action
dried yeast

50g (1¾oz) caster sugar

½ teaspoon fine salt

1 egg, lightly beaten

**For the filling:**

75g (2¾oz) butter, softened

50g (1¾oz) light brown
soft sugar

2 teaspoons ground cinnamon

½ teaspoon fine salt

**For the glaze:**

1 egg, lightly beaten

pearl or demerara sugar,
for sprinkling

Lightly oil a large baking sheet, or 9 pie tins about 8cm (3¼ inches) in diameter.

Put the milk in a small saucepan, add the cardamom and bring to just below boiling point. Turn off the heat, stir in the butter until melted and leave the mixture to stand until it is just warm.

Mix all the dry ingredients together in a large bowl. Make a well in the middle and add the egg, then stir in the warm milk mixture. Gradually mix until well combined and a soft sticky dough forms that comes away from the side of the bowl.

Turn the dough out on to a lightly oiled work surface (don't flour it) and knead by hand for 5 minutes. The dough will be very soft and sticky at first, but will become less sticky with kneading. Alternatively, use a stand mixer fitted with a dough hook.

Lightly oil a bowl and add the dough. Cover with clingfilm or a clean tea towel and leave to rise in a warm place for 30–60 minutes or until doubled in size.

While the dough is rising, make the filling. Beat all the ingredients together in a separate bowl until soft and easily spreadable.

Roll the dough out on a lightly floured surface to a rectangle measuring about 35 x 25cm (14 x 10 inches) and 3mm (¹/₈ inch) thick. Spread the cinnamon filling over the dough and, starting from

one of the long edges, roll the dough up tightly like a Swiss roll, ending with the seam underneath. Cut into 10 slices around 2.5cm (1 inch) thick.

Place on the baking sheet, leaving a small space between them, or in the individual tins or sections, and then cover and leave to prove in a warm place for about 30 minutes until the dough springs back when prodded gently.

For the glaze, brush the buns with the beaten egg and sprinkle with the sugar. Meanwhile, preheat the oven to 200°C (400°F), Gas Mark 6.

Bake the buns for 20–25 minutes until golden brown. Turn out on to a wire rack to cool for a while – delicious served warm.

# SOCIAL FOODIES
## – because what else would we be talking about?

**I nearly became a vegan last summer. We spent a few weeks in Sweden and were served so many vegetarian delicacies that meat suddenly seemed superfluous to me. And with all the enticing vegan food blogs and cookbooks coming out of the country right now, it's easy to see why I was tempted to go green all the way.**

The veggie trend is not exclusively Swedish, of course, but it is typical of the Swedes to go all the way, to read about every new trend and learn how to bake that most popular bread. And yes, maybe even try making homemade coconut yogurt. Not very *lagom*, is it? To understand the Swedish approach to food, you must consider its social role. With language very much a functional thing, used sparsely and never wasted purely for politeness, food is far more than the experience of hunger and fullness. For a people averse to small talk, food becomes a talking point as well as an activity in itself. Swedes talk about food, taste each other's food, share recipes or simply enjoy food in silence. We plan food, cook food and enjoy food. The volume is unimportant – the function and experience are key.

## Adding the *lagom* ingredient

From a *lagom* perspective, it actually makes a lot of sense. We all need to eat, and in incorporating the necessity into a sociable experience, perhaps by meeting up with neighbours for a Christmas sweets-making session or chopping veg together for a simple pasta dish when your friends are over, you add balance by way of both lower costs and fewer additives, in addition to a chance to truly be present in the moment. Potluck parties are hugely popular in Sweden, and picnics are part and parcel of the social life.

# THROWING A PICNIC
## – the cheap, easy and *lagom* way to party

I've been enjoying picnics for as long as I can remember. As kids, we mostly had them as part of kindergarten outings to the woods or in our garden in the summertime between games of hide and seek or hula hoops and somersaults. As I grew older, I started meeting friends in parks and by the lake for socializing whenever the weather allowed (sunshine is a holy thing for Swedes, not to be messed around with or taken for granted), and later still we brought cans of beer and guitars to the park for parties when the bars seemed too expensive or simply too claustrophobic.

Far from just being events of their own, picnics often complement a number of other Swedish activities, from midsummer get-togethers to playdates with children and ice skating on a frozen lake. Ask a Swede about the best part of downhill skiing holidays in the mountains, and they'll doubtless mention open sandwiches and a mug of hot chocolate on the sunny slopes. Not your traditional picnic, perhaps, but food prepared to be enjoyed outdoors nonetheless.

## MY FAVOURITE PICNIC?

A good park-based birthday bash. Forget soulless play centres or hordes of kids climbing the walls of your house. Forget big restaurant bookings and awkward splitting of bills. Serve up the delicacies yourself or ask your friends to do the potluck thing – with some bunting between trees and a guitar or portable speakers, a picnic party makes for an unpretentious but lovely event.

## Picnic thinking

What I love about picnics is the ease with which they can be arranged – the flexibility of the concept, whether you're packing up for a day at the beach or spontaneously hitting the park with some friends. Go all out with a homemade pasta salad, fruit salad, cake and a flask of coffee, or keep it simple with sandwiches. If you're the spontaneous kind, swing by the shop for some berries, hummus and bread. Have a blanket? Great. If not, your coat will do. Either way, you'll save a fortune compared with eating out, and you can't go wrong with sunshine, fresh air and friends.

"Sunshine is a holy thing for Swedes, not to be taken for granted."

# ELDERFLOWER CORDIAL

Elderflower is refreshing, summery and incredibly versatile – plus it's freely available in parks and fields if you fancy a foraging session (unless of course you're up for cultivating some yourself and gaining a beautiful addition to your allotment or garden). With a basic elderflower cordial in the pantry, you'll be ready to please children at birthday parties and adults craving cocktails alike (*see* the recipe opposite).

**Makes:** about 2 litres (3½ pints)

20 elderflower heads, shaken to remove any insects

3 lemons, sliced

25g (1oz) citric acid (available online)

1 litre (1¾ pints) water

1kg (2lb 4oz) granulated or caster sugar

Put the elderflower heads, lemon slices and citric acid in a large, heatproof bowl.

Put the water and sugar in a large saucepan and slowly bring to the boil over a low heat, stirring occasionally until the sugar has dissolved.

Pour the sugar syrup over the ingredients in the bowl and stir well, then leave to cool. Cover with clingfilm and leave to infuse overnight.

Strain the mixture through a sieve lined with muslin, then pour into sterilized airtight bottles, seal and store in a cool place for up to 6 months.

# ELDERFLOWER COOLER

**Whether it's picnic time or you're throwing a barbecue in the garden, your homemade Elderflower Cordial (*see* left) will come in handy for making a distinctive-tasting and refreshing drink. Adult party time? Add your white spirit of choice and enjoy!**

1 lemon

5 limes

a few sprigs of mint

ice cubes

Elderflower Cordial (*see* left)

cold water or soda water

Squeeze the juice of the lemon into a large jug or pitcher, then do the same with the limes and throw the squeezed-out fruits into the pitcher along with the mint sprigs and some cubes of ice.

Fill the jug with 1 part elderflower cordial to 10 parts water, or soda water if you prefer a fizzy drink, and stir to mix.

# SEEDED RYE BREAD

**From *smörgåsbord* spreads to open sandwiches and solid breakfasts, a good, healthy rye bread recipe is a must-have for any *lagom* enthusiast.**

**Makes:** 1 x 900g (2lb) loaf

sunflower oil, for oiling

250g (9oz) dark rye flour

250g (9oz) white rye flour, plus extra for dusting

2 teaspoons fine salt

500ml (18fl oz) boiling water

2 teaspoons fast-action dried yeast

2 tablespoons dark syrup or black treacle

75g (2¾oz) cracked rye or rye flakes

75g (2¾oz) sunflower seeds

75g (2¾oz) linseeds (flaxseeds)

Lightly oil a 900g (2lb) loaf tin.

Mix the flours and salt together in a large bowl. Pour over the measured boiling water and mix together into a thick, slightly crumbly paste. Leave to cool a little.

Add the dried yeast and syrup or treacle to the paste along with the cracked rye or rye flakes and most of the seeds, reserving some for the top. Stir in just enough water to bring the mixture together into a soft but not too sticky dough – about 2 tablespoons.

Turn the dough out on to a lightly floured work surface and knead the dough for about 5 minutes until it feels smooth and well combined. Alternatively, use a stand mixer fitted with a dough hook.

Shape the dough into a sausage shape roughly the same length as the loaf tin. Place in the prepared tin, brush the top of the loaf with water and sprinkle with the reserved seeds.

Cover with a damp clean cloth and leave in a warm, draught-free place for several hours, preferably overnight, until slightly risen – it won't double in size, but will rise by about a quarter.

When ready to bake, preheat the oven to 200°C (400°F), Gas Mark 6. Once hot, place a roasting tray half-filled with boiling water in the bottom of the oven. Bake the bread in the middle of the oven for about 35–40 minutes until the loaf is well browned on top and the base sounds hollow when tapped. Turn out on to a wire rack and leave to cool completely before slicing.

# NEW NORDIC CUISINE
## – going back to basics by foraging and growing your own

When René Redzepi and Claus Meyer's Copenhagen restaurant Noma was named the Best Restaurant in the World in 2014 for the fourth time in five years, the craze was a fact: New Nordic Cuisine would see all things Nordic grow in popularity across the globe – and quickly so. It's *lagom* in the extreme, boasting true enjoyment of and passion for food, enveloped by a sophisticated respect for nature's gifts and a moderate consumption of the same.

**DID YOU KNOW?**

There's a New Nordic Food Manifesto, designed in 2004 by Claus Meyer and endorsed by some of Scandinavia's most renowned chefs.

Among other things, the manifesto calls for foodies to reflect the changes of the seasons in their cooking and to combine the demand for good taste with modern knowledge of health and wellbeing.

Magnus Nilsson became somewhat of a pioneer: a robust man with an impressive beard serving up the food he'd grown, foraged and hunted with his own bare hands, in a cottage surrounded by nothing but mountains and woods. Sweden's current best chef according to industry rankings, Daniel Berlin, is of a similar school of thought and insists that cutting out the middle man is all about quality control, celebrating what we have and reflecting local, quality ingredients gastronomically.

## Join the slow-food movement

Hunting may raise ethical conundrums for some, but the grow-your-own trend is booming. Swedish apartment balconies are overflowing with tomatoes and rosemary plants, and gardens and allotments produce heaps of cabbages, courgettes and carrots. At a time of global warming and with food waste almost epidemic, there is something very *lagom* about growing your own and eating the fruits of your labour; it's short-travelled, it's affordable and you can plan your meals around what your allotment, veg patch, patio containers or grow sacks bring (*see* page 60).

## *ALLEMANSRÄTTEN*

The right of public access to nature is more generous in Sweden than anywhere else. To read more about the Swedish relationship to the great outdoors, *see* pages 102–5.

## TOP TIP

Hop on the bike, head for the woods or hedgerows and spend a whole day peacefully foraging, along with a *fika* break with a flask of hot chocolate or coffee and open sandwiches. Return home with your elderflowers for making cordial (*see* page 48), berries for making jam (*see* page 59) or a basket full of wild mushrooms (but only if you know your chanterelle from your toadstool), which you trim and wash before frying in butter, seasoning with sea salt and black pepper and serving on crispbread.

The foraging trend, meanwhile, is nothing new. During the summer holidays when the woods overflow with blueberries and after the back-to-school buzz when they shift into shades of golden brown with chanterelle mushrooms, Instagram feeds fill up with idyllic nature shots as urbanites and villagers alike flock to the forests. It can look staged and contrived to the foreign eye, but the love is real – perhaps linked to *allemansrätten* (*see* left), the right of access that makes all Swedish land the legitimate space of every citizen and guest, so ingrained into the Swedish consciousness that not enjoying the great outdoors seems like a mortal sin, especially if you choose to stay inside when the sun is shining. When nature serves up delicacies free of charge and preservatives, the Swedes go berserk. Foraging costs nothing, tops up the fresh air quota and comes with buckets of respect and gratitude for nature. How's that for a *lagom* downtime activity?

# Baking and brewing DIY

For a spot of indoors *lagom*, take up breadmaking – make your own sourdough starter if you're feeling ambitious or try the seeded rye bread recipe on page 50 – or start home brewing. The craft beer trend may be thriving across the globe, but Swedes are exceptionally keen in the DIY sense. There is an enthusiastic home-brewing community for anyone who needs advice, alongside ample brewing supply shops and well-established, respected beer festivals. Perfectly suited to the growing slow-food movement, both baking and brewing come with added benefits for a *lagom* lifestyle. Think community, craft and mindfulness (*see* page 114) – not a bad trio for the kitchen.

# THE END-OF-SUMMER BASH
## – a celebration of nature's gifts

Surely a gang of adults wearing silly party hats and singing "*snaps* (schnapps) songs" while slurping crayfish meat from their shells is the antithesis to *lagom*? Bear with me. The annual tradition of crayfish parties has its roots in an old Swedish ban on crayfish fishing due to fears that the shellfish would become extinct. Fishermen were not allowed to fish for crayfish during the months of June and July, or in some places before 7 August, and today the big crayfish première is celebrated widely across the country on 8 August.

Much like other Swedish traditions, crayfish parties benefit from dry weather, as they should preferably take place outdoors, ideally in a scenic setting near the water. But while huge servings of the red freshwater crustacean make the backbone of any crayfish party, ingredients including beer, a range of salads, bread, *snaps* and quiche are often added to the *smörgåsbord* buffet. Most importantly, friends and family get together in nature for an end-of-summer celebration of sorts – and they can talk about food, remember (*see* page 45)?

# VÄSTERBOTTEN CHEESE QUICHE

Quiches suit the *lagom* approach to eating not least because they work well as part of a buffet; being incredibly versatile, they're also perfect for bringing along to a potluck or picnic. This mature-cheese version is especially well suited to celebrations and special occasions.

**Serves:** 6 (or more if part of a buffet)

**For the pastry:**

175g (6oz) plain flour

125g (4½oz) cold salted butter, diced

2 tablespoons iced water

**For the filling:**

3 eggs

100ml (3½fl oz) milk

150ml (5fl oz/ ¼ pint) double cream

150g (5½oz) *Västerbottensost** cheese, grated

pinch of salt

freshly ground black pepper

Preheat the oven to 220°C (425°F), Gas Mark 7.

To make the pastry, put the flour and butter in a bowl, and rub with your fingertips until you have a crumbly texture. Stir in the measured water and bring the mixture together to make a smooth dough.

Press into a 24cm (9½-inch) round pie or quiche tin – if you have a loose-bottomed one, go for that. Prick the base of the pastry case with a fork and bake for 10–12 minutes until golden.

For the filling, whisk the eggs, milk and cream together in a bowl until well combined, then stir in the grated cheese. Season to taste with the salt and pepper. Pour the filling into the pastry case and bake for about 20 minutes until the filling is set. Leave to cool.

**Västerbottensost* is available in a number of well-stocked supermarket delis beyond Sweden, but if you can't get the real deal, try substituting your mature cheese of choice. Half mature Cheddar and half Parmesan works well.

# BLUEBERRY AND VANILLA JAM

**Depending on your whereabouts, you may neither have access to crayfish in August, nor be in need of a cheesy quiche to go with the crayfish bash. But blueberries are sure to be within reach, whether store-bought or, if you're fortunate enough, foraged locally.**

**Makes:** about 1 litre (1¾ pints)

900g (2lb) fresh blueberries

450g (1lb) jam sugar

4 tablespoons water

1 vanilla pod, halved lengthways

Place two saucers in the freezer.

Put all the ingredients in a large, heavy-based saucepan or preserving pan. Slowly bring to the boil over a low heat, stirring occasionally until the sugar has dissolved, then simmer for 10 minutes.

Increase the heat and boil rapidly for 15–20 minutes or until the jam reaches setting point. Test this by placing a large spoonful of the jam on a cold saucer and leave to cool for a few minutes. Gently push the jam with a clean finger; if it wrinkles, it has reached setting point.

Remove the pan from the heat and leave the jam to cool slightly. Remove and discard the vanilla pod, then ladle the jam into warmed sterilized airtight jars and seal. Store in a cool, dry, dark place.

# A LOVE OF ALLOTMENTS
## – a grow-your-own expert shares his top tips

**MEET JESPER JANSSON**

Jesper, 33, works as a subway driver and freelance animator. He lives in an apartment in the Stockholm suburb Bandhagen with *sambo* (meaning a partner you live with) Sofia, 35 and daughters Alva, 5 and Ellidhi (with whom he is currently on paternity leave) who is soon to turn one. Jesper and Sofia have had an allotment since 2010, when they felt the urge to try to become self-sufficient despite living in a big city.

If the multinational machinery of consumerist society is the antithesis of a sustainable lifestyle of moderate consumption, what could be more *lagom* than bringing food production closer to home, controlling what goes into the plants and choosing exactly what to grow? A seasoned allotmenteer imparts his wisdom.

## Allotment life – the impact

"In the beginning, we were very much focused on becoming self-sufficient and saving money on growing our own veg. We opted for large amounts of storable crops like potatoes and garlic and actually managed to be completely self-sufficient in terms of those items in the first few years.

"With time, the allotment has started to perform a much greater function. In addition to being a source of delicious ingredients, it's become an oasis for us to escape to – a place that's always there and easy to get to. It's an outlet for our desire to dig and do hands-on work, but also a place that's peaceful and scenic. The latter feels really good when we're tired of the apartment and the noise of the capital, and just want to be outdoors in a place that's still our own.

"On a typical day at the allotment, we'll not just work through our list of projects, like cutting the grass or sorting out a corner that's been neglected for too long, but also play with the kids and barbecue some veggie hotdogs."

## GROWING IN A TIGHT SPACE

No allotment just yet? Get started on the balcony or patio with herbs, chillies or different types of lettuce, all of which are relatively easy to grow in containers and require very little space. Or why not plant a few seed potatoes in a bucket?

## TIPS FROM THE EXPERT

### #1: Think first!

What do you want to do with your crop and how much will you be able to handle? There's nothing worse than having a big, beautiful harvest and realizing that you can't possibly eat it all or otherwise deal with it in time.

### #2: Mix in flowers

We always try to alternate rows of flowering plants with the rows of vegetable crops. It inhibits weeds, and if you manage to find the right "companion plants", they can protect certain sensitive crops from pests. Bonus: it makes a pretty display, too!

### #3: Try green fertilizing

Green fertilization is a way of giving the land a chance to recover by growing a variety of plants that bind different nutrients in the soil and suppress weeds after your crops have been harvested. The green manure, as such, is there not to feed you but to feed the soil.

### #4 Crop rotate

By rotating the crops you grow in various places each season, you can prevent soil erosion and control disease in your crops.

### #5: Winter sow

By winter sowing, which means planting seeds in mini pots and eventually bringing them outside in covered boxes, your plants will start growing earlier. It works with almost all types of plants and is useful in colder climates.

## The fruits of our labour

"We almost always grow garlic, mini cucumbers, tomatoes and potatoes, and often different types of kale and cabbage, as they're low maintenance and can survive far into the winters, which is nice as it prolongs the harvest period. Other favourites are pumpkin and courgette, beetroot and other root vegetables, radishes and lettuce, all of which are easy to grow and suit the Swedish climate.

"We also have some raised beds with currants, gooseberries, Jerusalem artichokes and the various herbs that last through the winter like thyme, chives, mint and tarragon, and we tend to let the nasturtium climb up our pergola, as the flowers are really pretty and tasty, too."

# EVERYTHING IN MODERATION

## – on being thrifty, enjoying sweets and taking breakfast seriously

If you don't fit the New Nordic brief and have no intention of growing your own vegetables, how can you cultivate a *lagom* relationship to food in your everyday life? Trust the Swedes to provide some clues.

### *Pyttipanna* and loving your leftovers

If you're in search of a gourmet experience, run a mile. If you want a quick and easy mid-week meal that minimizes your food waste and saves you a few quid along the way, *pyttipanna* is your friend. Their love of leftovers is the ultimate proof that Swedes aren't real food snobs after all; not only will they happily serve up *Snabbmakaroner* (macaroni that is ready in three minutes) and yesterday's chopped-up hotdogs for dinner, but they also even have a national dish based on nothing but leftovers. Take potatoes, meatballs, carrots, sausages or whatever is in the refrigerator and chop it up small, then fry in butter and top with a fried egg or beetroot. *Et voilà – pyttipanna* is served, a brand-new dish using nothing but leftovers.

In other thrifty news, I've been known to whip up a veggie Bolognese complete with whatever's in the refrigerator or pantry – I'll see your carrots and chopped tomatoes and raise you celery, onions, red split lentils and a spoonful of nut butter. It's creativity and low expectations in equal measure, and the pay-off is huge savings in terms of time, money and the environment alike.

### *Lördagsgodis* – the once-a-week treat

Let's get one thing straight: there's nothing *lagom* about *lördagsgodis*, the Saturday tradition of filling deep paper

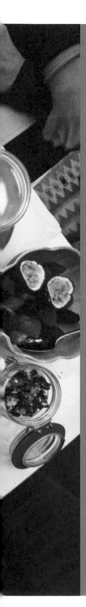

bags with pick-'n'-mix sweets only to finish them all in one short sitting. In many ways, it's the definition of a pig-out, and the Swedes love it. But put the Saturday sweets into context and you'll see that it's really about an attitude of everything in moderation. If you save your intake of crisps for your *fredagsmys* (*see* page 24) and sweets for your *lördagsgodis*, perhaps you're not doing so badly after all.

## Breakfast – the most important meal of the day

Of all the culinary culture shocks I've experienced since leaving the motherland, the structure of meals throughout the day is probably the most confusing. Swedish home economics classes, compulsory in schools, hammer home the message about *tallriksmodellen*, "the plate model", which preaches that every meal be made up of specific amounts of grains and carbohydrates, protein and fruit and veg, alongside the perhaps most fundamental of Swedish food doctrines – that breakfast is the most important meal of the day. Forget sugary cereals and white toast. Ignore recent fads about cutting out breakfast for weight loss. The *lagom* way is to eat well throughout the day – not too little and not too much – and keep your blood sugar levels as consistent as you can. That includes a solid breakfast, be it with porridge and berries or wholegrain bread and eggs. Start the day as you intend to go on!

## *Mellis* or the *lagom* snack

After their solid breakfast, Swedes have *mellis* – a substantial snack – and then a cooked lunch, followed by another *mellis* and a cooked dinner. Each *mellis* can be replaced or complemented by *fika*, naturally. The world's greatest mystery to Swedish adults is how children elsewhere can eat nothing but sandwiches and crisps for lunch at school and yet have the energy to learn anything at all. Of course, they clearly do, but it's so counter-intuitive to Swedes that they still can't quite believe it. Eating little and often is not a fad in Sweden – it's completely normal, as long as what you eat is cooked and moderate. You don't need eight potatoes when the next healthy snack is less than two hours away.

# CELEBRATE LIKE A SWEDE
## – with homemade, seasonal treats

With *lördagsgodis* and *fika* in mind, it comes as no surprise that Swedes know how to celebrate. Think of it as the balancing out of all that healthy, wholegrain bread they've had; as the perfectly considered way to mark life's big events, not by endless consumption of ready-made foods but by making use of nature's gifts and the local culinary heritage. Much like the New Nordic Cuisine pioneers and their talk of seasonal cooking (*see* page 52), Swedish food traditions are very often linked to the seasons and specific festivities.

**DID YOU KNOW?**

Swedes consume approximately 20 million *semlor*, or Lenten buns, every year.

# STRAWBERRY MERINGUE CAKE

**My mother's strawberry meringue cake will always take me right back to my childhood birthdays, but this Swedish classic works just as well for a midsummer celebration or any summery party or *fika*.**

**Serves:** 10–12

**For the sponge cake:**

sunflower oil, for oiling

3 egg yolks

150g (5½oz) caster sugar

1 tablespoon vanilla sugar*

75ml (5 tablespoons) milk

50g (1¾oz) butter, melted and cooled

150g (5½oz) plain flour

2 teaspoons baking powder

**For the meringue:**

4 egg whites

150g (5½oz) caster sugar

65g (2¼oz) blanched almonds, chopped

**For the filling and topping:**

400ml (14fl oz) double or whipping cream

400g (14oz) strawberries, hulled and sliced

Preheat the oven to 180°C (350°F), Gas Mark 4. Line two 20cm (8 inch) round cake tins with baking parchment and lightly brush with oil.

For the sponge, whisk the egg yolks, caster sugar and vanilla sugar (or vanilla extract) together in a large bowl until fluffy and pale in colour. Then whisk in the milk and cooled melted butter. Sift the flour and baking powder together into the bowl, then gently fold into the whisked mixture. Spread the batter out evenly in the prepared tins.

For the meringue, in a separate large, super-clean, grease-free bowl, whisk the egg whites until they form firm peaks, then whisk in the sugar until the mixture is thick and glossy, which will result in a nicely chewy meringue. Spread the meringue mixture across the cake batter and sprinkle with the chopped almonds. Bake for 20 minutes until golden.

Let the cakes cool in the tins, then remove and peel off the lining paper.

Lightly whip the cream with a whisk until it forms soft peaks. Place one cake half on a plate and top with just over half the cream and half the sliced strawberries. Top with the other cake half and add the remaining cream and strawberries.

*Vanilla sugar is commonly used in baking in northern Europe, but you can substitute it here with a few drops of vanilla extract.

# GLÖGG
## – mulled wine

Advent is a very special time in Sweden. During the four Sundays in the build-up to Christmas, Swedes start lighting candles, adorning their windows with star lights and Advent candelabra and baking in preparation for the festive season. While Christmas itself can often feel like one big saturated, overwhelming feast, with most people maxed out on everything from food to carols before it even begins, Advent is its more restrained *lagom* cousin. It will come as no surprise that many Swedes actually prefer Advent to the big day itself. Come the end of November every year, I am usually more than ready to get into the Christmas spirit – but that can't happen without *glögg*.

**Serves:** about 15 small cups

75cl (1 pint 6fl oz) bottle red wine

250ml (9fl oz) unsweetened apple juice

2 small pieces of dried root ginger or 2.5cm (1 inch) piece of peeled fresh ginger

1 piece of bitter orange peel

2 cinnamon sticks

10 cloves

½ teaspoon cardamom pods

**To serve**

orange slices

cinnamon sticks

star anise

raisins and whole blanched almonds (optional)

Put all the ingredients, except those to serve, in a saucepan and heat over a low heat until you see steam rising from the top of the mixture, stirring frequently and being careful not to let it boil.

Turn the heat off, cover the pan and leave to sit overnight.

When ready to serve, reheat gently as before and serve in little cups with orange slices, a cinnamon stick, a star anise and sprinkle with a few raisins and blanched almonds, if liked.

Cheers or *skål!*

# Styling lagom:
## design, fashion & interiors

"There is no bad weather, only bad clothes," goes an old Swedish proverb. Functionalism is a constant throughout the Swedish design heritage, from the catwalks to the design boutiques, and yet Swedes manage to make everything look so stylish. How?

3

# THE SWEDISH DESIGN HERITAGE
## – sleek eco functionalism all the way

"To design a desk which may cost £1,000 is easy for a furniture designer, but to design a functional and good desk which shall cost only £50 can only be done by the very best," Ingvar Kamprad, founder of IKEA, famously said. With clever flat-pack furniture and tips and tricks for how to make urban family life work on little more than 60 square metres, the Swedish furniture giant IKEA has spread across the globe, but I've come to realize that its reputation is far from consistently strong.

### Designed to last

The idea often prevalent outside of Sweden that cheap equals poor quality has contributed to a view of IKEA as the stronghold of a trend-sensitive throw-away design culture. Having grown up surrounded by the manufacturer's record-selling Billy bookcases, some of which were at home when I was born and passed on to me at 18 when I moved out, I don't recognize that image at all. As Kamprad also once said: "Waste of resources is a mortal sin at IKEA."

But Sweden's design heritage goes back a long way before the flat-pack giant. Names such as Bruno Mathsson and Astrid Sampe made waves in the post-war era, and a vein of socially oriented design grew strong. In 1993, the sustainability ethos became a fact as Norrgavel opened its doors, heralding a humanist, organic, existentialist approach to eco-labelled furniture made of wood.

Swedish high-street fashion giant H&M has more than 4,000 shops globally, and you can recycle your clothes in every single one of them to get vouchers toward your next purchase.

# Fashion follows the *lagom* suit

In the world of fashion, meanwhile, the full range of designs from affordable to exclusive are represented by renowned brands including H&M, Weekday, WeSC, Acne Studios, Tiger of Sweden, Rodebjer, COS, Boomerang and Filippa K. Known primarily for a similar design expression as the furniture and interiors pioneers, the fashion scene is also huge, especially recently, on unisex and agender. In this industry, too, the throw-away attitude is actively resisted, with many brands introducing more durable and organic ranges and allowing customers to hire catwalk garments.

H&M, which is occasionally dismissed with similar criticisms as those directed against IKEA, has in fact since 2011 been phasing out the use of hazardous chemicals with the aim of reaching zero discharge by 2020. Through reuse and recycling, the brand is hoping to become a fully circular enterprise. Over at the Swedish Fashion Council, another step toward a sustainable industry was taken this year with the launch of a Swedish Fashion Ethical Charter. Covering the entire industry – from modelling and advertising agencies to stylists and designers – the initiative is unique and aims to provide guidelines for a more socially sustainable industry.

# A sustainable legacy

Modern Swedish design is *lagom* in more than one way. It perfectly balances an innovative, forward-thinking streak with a proud heritage, and it puts functionality and sustainability first – regardless of the price. What Kamprad said is food for thought. If affordability and quality aren't mutually exclusive, perhaps the throw-away culture came about as a result of affordable products and not in response to their lacking in quality; if you look after those Billy bookcases, they may well last for life.

# DRESSING LAGOM STYLE
## – the uber-cool, the nature lover and the *kulturtant*

Being one myself, I've become an expert at spotting Swedes abroad. They come in different guises, but the majority have a few things in common, most crucially that functionality and comfort always come first. Looking stylish is all well and good, but dressing *lagom* is just as much about making it easy for yourself and feeling comfortable as it is about fitting in in the most sophisticated of ways. Suffice to say that garments labelled as requiring hand washing and shoes made of plastic are likely to be left on the shelves.

### LYKKE LI BUN

Top off your look with a simple topknot, dubbed "the Lykke Li bun" a few years ago after the Swedish singer who popularized it. Any shoulder-length or longer cut can easily be manipulated into this simple, sleek style to add an effortlessly cool look.

In Stockholm, unsurprisingly, buns are for men, too – yes, that's a man bun!

### The über-cool urbanite

Take the dark, sleek, classic simplicity of ultra-refined brand Filippa K and combine it with the bold cuts and prints of the slightly more youthful yet so stylish Monki, and what you get is the hip but handy look of about half the people frequenting the coolest bars in Stockholm's trendy Södermalm. Think comfortable, loose shapes, a colour scheme in mostly black with the odd attention-grabbing print or statement scarf, some big jewellery, often peroxide-blonde hair and bright-red lipstick and comfortable, walking-friendly shoes – say leather brogues or hip sneakers.

Behind this trendy look is a capsule wardrobe of black basics that work with everything, topped up with a handful of garments that stand out. Nothing uncomfortable or restrictive – just stuff you love. With a wardrobe like this, you can opt for quality over quantity, prioritizing some of the organic cotton ranges that are popping up in many high-street chains.

# The sporty nature lover

Few brands embody the Swedish love of the great outdoors like Fjällräven, most widely known for the iconic Kånken backpack, which comes in a range of bright and earthy colours. A comfortable pair of jeans and a quality windcheater complete the look, and teamed with a white or light-blue shirt, you can even bring it to the office.

An appetite for quality functional and outdoor clothes has resulted in a range of Swedish brands to leave you spoiled for choice, including Haglöfs, Didriksons, Craft and Peak Performance. WeSC, every skateboarder's and snowboarder's staple brand, takes a street-smart approach to the quality-conscious sporty look. No need to compromise on edginess to dress for the elements, in other words.

# The culture lady

*Lagom* doesn't have to be middle-of-the-road – especially not if you're a middle-aged woman. With eco brand Gudrun Sjödén showing the way, thousands of Swedish women have found self-expression in the *kulturtant* (loosely translating as "culture lady") style, typically made up of bright but nature-inspired colours, linen and other natural materials, and layers upon layers of loose fabrics. Just add stripy tights *à la* Pippi Longstocking, scarves aplenty, big finger rings or pendants and shoes or boots from ECCO or Camper – or, for bonus points, head for Stockholm's own Knulp.

While the *kulturtant* look is a far cry from the sophisticated Södermalm style, it is *lagom* in a number of ways, perhaps mostly in celebrating comfort and green thinking without restricting freedom of expression. Who said pink doesn't go with orange? The sustainable capsule wardrobe works just as well with garments of all the colours of the rainbow.

# TIPS FROM THE STYLIST
## – on "comfy chic", upcycling and a bold approach to *lagom*

**ANNA LIDSTRÖM**

Anna is an award-winning designer and stylist who runs Another Studio, and works as a consultant, designer, stylist and lecturer in the areas of advertising, fashion and home furnishing as well as the arts. For more inspiration, check out @anotherblog.se on Instagram

**Without access to Swedish fashion outlets, there are ways to apply a *lagom* mindset to dressing with style. You don't even have to blend in – unless you want to.**

## On Swedish style and "comfy chic"

"As a fashion nation, we're very good at a comfortable, basic style with varied details and understated cuts. Our clothes are designed to allow us to pop outside quickly, so we've become experts at dressing practically. We stand out the *lagom* way – a tiny bit, but not too much. At home, the trend-conscious part of the population is somewhat like a monochrome mass, but if you go abroad you can immediately spot a Swede in a crowd – in that context, the low-key style almost seems extravagant.

## On *lagom* fashion

"What is cultural status for us Swedes? For a long time, it's been about not expressing status at all. Swedes have rarely used garments as a canvas for colours, patterns or messages – that visual luxury you see in Italian fashion history. We've never had big fashion houses to splash out on; here, functionalism and frugality have always been virtues. Clothes are viewed as consumables, good-to-have items. They're for everyone, and things that are for everyone must be *lagom* – not too colourful, not too crazy. It can be a bit boring, but also quite liberating; it's like casual Friday every day, and everyone can relax more.

## TOP TIPS FROM THE STYLIST

### #1: Give your wardrobe a facelift

As the fashion scene moves on and your style with it, the way you look at your clothes might change. Review the contents of your wardrobe regularly, but don't just focus on passing things on. You might rediscover an old skirt and realize that it works perfectly as a quirky petticoat for an old dress that needed a lift. Take snapshots of yourself and sleep on it, and that will help you evaluate your finds.

### #2: Dust off that sewing machine

We're throwing away our pianos and sewing machines, and with them we're throwing out the skills and knowledge. Learn to sew on a button, then a zip and eventually you might even dare to adapt an old garment into something new. There are plenty of great tutorials on YouTube!

### #3: Re-evaluate your capsule wardrobe

Having a base of useful clothes you love to wear over and over again is great, but we should move away from this idea of a set capsule wardrobe for everyone. Maybe your perfect base is 11 floral-print dresses, while someone else is all about a reliable range of waxed coats and trainers.

### #4: Be brave and dare to "ugly match"

I often talk about "ugly matching", that it can be liberating to try out something, get it wrong and learn to live with it. It's only by experimenting that you'll truly discover your own personal expression and learn to trust your instinct with regard to style. Who knows, you might find that you love something that current trends would dismiss as ugly!

## Saving as a virtue

"There's this inherent celebrating of frugality in Sweden. We like affordable clothes because it's a bit vulgar to splash out. But there's a balance to be struck, because our respect for material things is directly linked to their price – we're more likely to fix a broken zip on a coat from Acne than on one from an affordable high-street chain. It's too easy to buy cheap and just replace everything.

## On upcycling and creativity

"Most of us just want to renew ourselves and our style. There's been a huge trend recently in making the most of what you already have, allowing you to follow fast-changing trends by reinventing yourself using your own wardrobe finds. This kind of remixing is an interesting way to combine moderate living with that desired renewal, and it's the way forward for both designers and consumers."

# ADOPTING THE FUNCTIONALIST MINDSET
## – on a practical wardrobe and rational shopping

## How to go functional

### #1: Care for your clothes

To survive rain and freezing cold, you need quality stuff – but to get quality, you need to splash out. Think long term and really look after your clothes. Whether it's rewaxing that five-year-old coat or spraying those boots, a bit of care will pay off.

### #2: Forget fads

Thinking long term means forgetting about short-lived trends and learning to buy things you really like. Not to say you can't be on trend. Colourful rainwear, for example, has never gone out of style yet it still keeps you dry.

### #3: Put comfort first

Nothing ruins a day like cut heels or bleeding toes, so buy shoes that are truly comfortable. Then you're more likely to opt for walking, too – the perfect *lagom* way to get both fresh air and light exercise.

You may have heard of the Swedish proverb declaring: "There is no bad weather, only bad clothes." Swedes jokingly refer to this when chatting to tourists about the freezing winters, but the attitude is very real indeed. Swedes have perfected the art of living in sub-zero conditions and weathering extreme seasonal changes. Everyone knows that the secret to staying warm is layering it up; everyone knows that a layer of wool goes closest to the skin. Call it a *lagom* approach to survival – making your home stylish and cosy enough to enjoy staying in, but ensuring that your wardrobe is up to the challenge when it's time to face the elements.

It took me months to get used to living without a thermometer in the window when I first moved abroad. Swedes have a wardrobe per season, often along with an attic storage system for replacing one seasonal box with the next. As such, there really is no bad weather – because with a thermometer in the window, you can make sure you always choose the appropriate clothes to wear.

# STORAGE, BABY
## – create a sense of space

**TOP TIP**

To save floor space and make cleaning quick and easy, use your walls for storage. Think sleek shelving units, magnetic knife and key holders and wall-mounted shoe storage.

**DID YOU KNOW?**

The iconic String shelves (*pictured* left) came about when Swedish publisher Bonnier launched a competition in 1949 to provide Swedes with a practical shelving system to enable them to buy more books. Nisse Strinning's design won and has since become a timeless Swedish design classic.

It's no coincidence that one of the most famous pieces of furniture by renowned Swedish design brand Svenskt Tenn is a cabinet with 19 drawers, Josef Frank's Cabinet 881; that one of the longest-standing items by flat-pack giant IKEA is the Billy bookcase; and that one of the most sought-after items on Swedish second-hand furniture sites is String shelves (*see* below left). Swedish design is known for minimalism and clean lines, and storage and decluttering are crucial components of the sleek look.

Open surfaces provide a sense of space, not just in the literal sense but for your mind, too. From wall-to-wall bookshelves to clever under-stair storage units, Swedes really know how to declutter the *lagom* way. This means providing perfect displays for plants, flea market finds and favourite books while keeping tables and other surfaces clear, simultaneously making sure you stow away cables, keys and other items that are easily left lying around to immediately cancel out your best minimalist efforts.

# A LAGOM HOME
## – a home stylist's thoughts on a sustainable, happy home

**JULIA BRANTING**

Julia is a Stockholm-based freelance home stylist and visual merchandizer.

We've touched on storage, but what can you do to bring that *lagom* balance into your home besides decluttering? A real pro who spends most of her time styling homes for sale shares her top tips.

## On Swedish interior decoration

"The Swedish style is generally very bright – lots of white, maybe grey and some wood details. Think open-plan layout and a design classic like the Lamino armchair. The feature wall embodies the *lagom* approach to interiors: you go for one wall in a different colour or wallpaper, because doing the whole room would be a bit much. One wall is *lagom*.

## On the eco interior trend

"There's a range of brands working with sustainability and taking their responsibility in that regard. Buy from them – it's often great-quality stuff, too. Sweden has a huge second-hand market (*see* page 94), and there are also a number of really good websites for buying and selling old furniture and interior design items in good condition. You can also get eco-certified paint and wallpaper. It's a big trend at the moment, and I hope it's here to stay.

## On storage

"It's easy to think of storage as a necessary evil, but you can make it part of the room. Think an entire wall of shelves, cupboards put together in a stylistic modular combination or drawer units under the bed. Making the best use of height is always a good option.

## On mood-enhancing interiors

"Pick a neutral base with furniture and colours you really like. Then you can change and move details around depending on your mood or the season. Decluttering is key to minimizing stress. One of my top tips is to create a favourite corner for relaxing and recharging."

# LAGOM COSY
## – on embracing crafts, colours and true cosiness

### TOP TIP #1

Take up knitting or another portable craft. The calming effect is addictive, train journeys will pass faster than ever and your home will gain a personal touch that's hard to beat with store-bought design.

### TOP TIP #2

Rummage through your parents' or grandparents' attics and sheds, and get that sandpaper out. The simplest of coffee tables, a rickety old stool or a battered picture frame can easily be fashioned into a charming, characterful interior detail with an interesting story to tell.

While white simplicity is a safe bet when it comes to creating a minimalist Nordic home, recent trends show a backlash tendency celebrating earthier colours and kitsch. Think walls painted dark green, embroidered cushions and shelves chock full of old, decorative items – cosy, perhaps, but not exactly what first springs to mind when trying to strike that *lagom* balance.

## The earthy approach

With countless people taking up knitting, vintage boutiques overflowing with quality arts and crafts and statement colours being all the rage, interior design is going organic and snug – and the earthiness is twofold. By rummaging through your granny's attic, upcycling furniture from your childhood and getting crafty, you can add character to your home without consuming much at all. Behold a comfy, heart-warming home with an unspoiled, happy environment as a bonus.

## Reaping the benefits

There's a back-to-basics movement brewing, and the benefits are endless. Knitting and crocheting are both portable and calming. A home-knitted blanket adds a personal touch to your home, while inherited handicraft items, picture frames and old lamps provide a sense of heritage. If your grandparents were the chucking-everything-away kind and you'd rather catch up on blog posts than spend your journey to work knitting, there are always vintage shops and flea markets (*see page 94*). They may tell less of a personal story, but the environmental gains and cosiness factor remain.

# THE LOPPIS TREND
## – fresh air, friends and sustainable bargains

To most urbanites, flea markets are hipster-dense weekend destinations in the trendiest city quarters. To most Swedes, they are something quite different. Going to a *loppis,* short for *loppmarknad,* often entails breathing in bags of fresh country air in picturesque surroundings dotted with red barns. Providing an opportunity to do something simple but different with your friends and taking the consumption imperative out of the shopping experience, a flea market crawl, or *loppisrunda,* is the perfect *lagom* recreational activity.

**TOP TIP**

Turn a trip to your local flea market into a day out. Even if you don't manage to pick up a bargain, you can be sure to find plenty of inspiration. Most importantly, it's a nice way to spend quality time with your friends.

## Join the slow-shopping movement

A good *loppis* comes with the chance of finding real bargains: from rare china to design classics. You will probably have to look through tables of junk, but that's all part of the experience – and part of the joy. Buying items in a design shop is easy; finding them surrounded by dusty old knick-knacks takes determination and patience.

Most importantly, however, the *loppis* experience is about more than shopping. The charm of the Swedish *loppis* craze is everything that surrounds it: a day out with friends, fresh air and nature, maybe jumping on the bike for an extended ride out of town and, naturally, enjoying some coffee and cinnamon buns in a barn café.

Research shows that the happiness that comes with buying things is exceptionally short-lived. As such, there's beauty and pleasure in allowing the shopping process to take its time, making it more about the experience than the end purchase. If you come home empty-handed, your home will remain the same, but you'll feel refreshed and your environmental footprint will be near invisible.

# Feeling lagom:
## health & wellbeing

Discover the Swedish approach to exercise, learn to love the great outdoors and find out why feeling *lagom* is the secret to sustainable happiness.

4

# UNPRETENTIOUS EXERCISE
## – the movement that's taking over Sweden

**DID YOU KNOW?**

With in excess of 526,000 members, Friskis&Svettis has won the hearts of more than 5% of the Swedish population.

**TOP TIP**

If you suffer from a dearth of Friskis&Svettis clubs in your area or a shortage of neighbours, there are other ways to get some *lagom*, unpretentious exercise into your life. From belly dancing to circus classes and park workout sessions, find what floats your boat – and enjoy it!

Imagine strolling through one of Sweden's many city parks on a sunny Sunday morning and suddenly hearing the latest guitar hit turned up to the max. What you're likely to find the other side of a few trees is not a small festival, but a bunch of people of different ages and sizes jumping up and down, waving their arms in sync.

Friskis&Svettis is one of Sweden's largest sports organizations, with over half a million members across scores of voluntary-run clubs, now also in places such as London, Paris and Brussels. The values behind it are all about feeling good and having fun, and the classes have none of the prestige of a traditional gym. In a lot of ways, this organization is *lagom* epitomized. It's affordable, sociable, flexible and healthy, and if you make the effort to turn up, no one will judge you for your lack of appropriate gym wear or laugh if you get the moves wrong.

## Community initiatives

The spirit of putting fun first is alive and well beyond Friskis&Svettis. A friend of mine, a mother of three in a small town in central Sweden, recently posted on social media about her neighbourhood's new initiative: an outdoor neighbours' fitness club. Meeting on the green a couple of evenings a week, the neighbours take turns to devise sessions, from military-style training to jogging and casual football. Knowing that the other neighbours are all heading out, they're less likely to take a rain check – and as a reward they get an hour of socializing along with that much-needed endorphin buzz. When was the last time you asked your neighbour out for a power walk?

# RETHINKING TRANSPORT
## – enjoying the journey the *lagom* way

There's a family story I'll never forget about my dad cycling 10 or so kilometres (more than 6 miles) to buy what was then dubbed the market's best coffeemaker, on special offer. After queueing for an hour to nab the last machine and swinging by the off-licence, he returned to his bike to find he had a flat tyre. Even with a big coffeemaker and heavy bag of craft beer in tow – and despite it starting to rain – at no point did he even consider catching the bus home. Suffice to say, he made it back – soaked but with his Swedish pride intact.

### Take the scenic route

You could look at transport as a means to an end, with a five-minute drive by far the most effective solution. But the *lagom* approach turns dead time into an experience, the need to get from A to B being a door to endless possibilities. So what if your town lacks a well-planned pedestrian lane network? Take the road less travelled! Gain exercise, enjoy some views you never knew you had, and save money while you're at it – all in a perfectly environmentally friendly way.

My father would see an over-crowded car as a challenge, as a ticket to a bike journey he otherwise might never have considered. He has been known to walk to the shop in the lashing rain more than once, despite not needing anything particularly urgently and despite being offered a lift. There is Swedish pride in that – in avoiding the car, consuming nothing but energy and fresh air, making the journey in itself useful. Add the fact that you can discover new neighbourhoods and pretty and peculiar houses, and even my mother will get on board.

# OUTDOOR LIFESTYLE GLOSSARY
## – clues to the *lagom* approach to exercise and the great outdoors

The Swedish love of and respect for nature goes beyond a keenness to exercise in parks and travel by foot. Decluttered, well-designed homes wouldn't be *lagom* unless complemented by a healthy dose of fresh air and outdoor fun. The following words provide some clues as to how Swedes have managed to strike that balance.

### Sportlov

I didn't know what "half-term" meant when I first moved to Ireland. Eventually I figured out that they were talking about *sportlov* – yes, "sports break" is what it's called in Sweden. *Sportlov* has its roots in war times, when pupils were given a week off to save on the costs of heating up the schools. Activities, typically winter sports and suchlike, were arranged, and the continuation of the sports breaks was justified by pointing to the many germs that were going around at that time of year. These breaks became a way to prevent the spread of infections. (Remember *Vabruari*? – *see* page 29.)

Today, *sportlov* is just a break like any other, but while the holiday activities can't be regulated and there's nothing to say that you must spend yours outside, many Swedes honour the tradition and take this opportunity to enjoy outings together, perhaps on the cross-country skiing tracks or out playing in the snow. Roughly halfway between the indulgent holidays of Christmas and Easter, it provides a bit of balance by way of fresh air and physical activity, along with that *lagom* attitude of embracing all kinds of weather conditions. There's no bad weather, only bad clothes, right?

### Motion

Type the Swedish word *motion* into a translation tool and it will bring up English equivalents like "exercise" and "motion". Interestingly, it means neither but a hard-to-describe blend of the two. *Motion* is as untranslatable as *lagom*, and it tells just as much of a tale about Swedish culture.

If your bus breaks down two stops before you're meant to get off, you might say that it's fine because you'll get some *motion* after all. Perhaps you've started going for a half-hour walk before work; you're not really exercising as such, but you certainly *motionerar*. The verb *motionera* implies that movement is taking place, and it's an altogether good, healthy kind of movement. With *motion*, your pulse is raised and you might even break a sweat, but the word doesn't work as a description of that kickboxing class or training for a marathon. No, it's a *lagom* kind of exercise.

The fact that the word, to most Swedes, evokes images of being out in nature speaks volumes, too. It doesn't take a genius to see that swimming in a lake or strolling through the woods is good for both heart and mind, yet the often-gentle nature of *motion* means that we're unlikely to make time for it – it's not hard core enough to be worthwhile. That's where a *lagom* culture with *lagom* traditions comes in handy: it makes *motion* an integrated part of a healthy lifestyle.

## Friluftsliv

Another untranslatable word, *friluftsliv* is an old Nordic philosophy of outdoor life. It describes recreational and leisure activities that take place outdoors, formally organized or otherwise, and makes a great contribution to your *sportlov*. Those with a rich *friluftsliv* would get plenty of *motion*, too – think time in the woods, bird watching, keen foraging (*see* page 54) or even camping in the wild. Other than the deification of all things outdoors, there's nothing extreme about this – just a perfectly *lagom* way to get out and about, disconnect from the web and connect with nature. Grab that Fjällräven backpack (*see* page 80–1) and those trekking boots and you're good to go!

## Allemansrätten

I seem to keep coming back to this one, and there's a reason: *allemansrätten* is about so much more than the right not to be kicked out of your tent when you're out camping with your family. This is a constitutional right to access nature (*see* page 54), and bar camping in someone's private garden, you have near-unrestricted access and can go swimming, cycling and picking wild flowers at will. Yet in line with the *lagom* ethos, this freedom comes with certain responsibilities – "Do not disturb, do not destroy", so the law demands. A very healthy compromise, don't you think?

# EMBRACING THE OUTDOORS
## – activities for every mood and season

From a law defending your right to access to nature (*see* page 105), to a proverb declaring that there is no such thing as bad weather (*see* page 86), Sweden's love of the outdoors manifests itself in many different ways – and with outdoor activities designed for every season, there's plenty of inspiration if you want to get your *friluftsliv* on (*see* page 105).

## Set yourself a challenge

Fancy a team sport? Go old school with ice hockey or football, or try a quiet round of *kubb*, also dubbed "Viking chess" (*see* opposite). For solo outings, get on those cross-country skis or explore the woods with some trail running. If you're looking for an adrenaline kick, try out rafting or challenge your friends to a proper snowball battle (*see* left).

## The laid-back or contemplative alternatives

If you want to really kick back, organize a barbecue and invite a few friends over – maybe even get the inflatable pool out for the kids. For the ultimate moment of mindfulness, bring a blanket to the park along with a book and some yoga pants. Or in the winter, make yourself a flask of hot chocolate and plant yourself in a sunny, wind-free spot and close your eyes.

### SNOWBALL FIGHT, ANYONE?

*Yukigassen* is a snowball-fighting tournament that originated in Japan but also has a base in *Luleå* in northern Sweden, where the Swedish Championships take place every year.

The game is played on a court between two teams of seven players each, and players are eliminated when hit with snowballs. There are special *yukigassen* helmets with shields, and 90 snowballs are made in advance.

For those keen on a battle but in warmer climates – water guns at the ready...

## *KUBB* IT UP!

*Kubb,* or Viking chess, is a game that's staged on a playing field involving wooden blocks, the task being to knock over the other team's blocks, or *kubbs,* before finally knocking down the king block in the middle. This is the perfect game for lazy days in the park or as a birthday picnic activity.

# NO DRAMA
## – on feeling it all and raising well-adjusted people

In the 2017 World Happiness Report, Sweden came in at number nine – respectable yet not exactly resounding. But let's add a few more metrics to the equation. In terms of trust, Sweden ranks exceptionally highly, and that's consistent over time. According to the OECD Better Life Index, Sweden scores highly in most aspects relating to wellbeing, including particularly high scores in the categories of health, life satisfaction, safety, work–life balance and the environment. Whatever the situation as to happiness in its most raw and explicit sense, we can safely assume that the average Swede enjoys a highly sustainable happiness of sorts.

### A *lagom* outlook on life

"If you're always having fun, you won't notice that you're having fun, so you have to be bored sometimes, too," says Swedish children's book character Alfons Åberg. You'll have to look long and hard to find a more *lagom* outlook on life. Beyond the realm of children's fiction, there are psychologists and researchers who agree with Alfons, not only suggesting that acknowledging the complexity of life is essential to psychological wellbeing, but even pointing out that an overly rosy mindset can lead to complacency and a risk of ignoring dangers. Swedes are probably described as a well-adjusted bunch more often than they're portrayed as being extremely happy, so maybe we're on to something here.

### Nudity and drama queens

So what can we learn from Alfons? The essence of a *lagom* approach to feelings is in embracing them all and not giving undue importance to any one emotion. And when you de-dramatize fears and emotional impulses, taboos start to seem nonsensical and it becomes easier to talk to people about even the difficult stuff.

Take sex and nudity, for example. A huge number of Swedish children grow up reading *KP* or *Kamratposten* (meaning "Paper Pal"), a children's magazine that has since 1892 been broaching subjects to do with mental, physical and sexual health in an approachable way. And then there is the 1960s children's literary figure Totte, more recently made into a cartoon, who is allowed to get undressed with his friend Malin to see how their bodies differ.

Embracing a *lagom* emotional life has little to do with snapchatting about your inner fears and lowest moments (while Swedes have started to move beyond the Law of Jante's condemnation of people who stand out and speak to their strengths – *see* page 11 – a remnant of it is still very much present in a strong dislike of drama queens) or walking around the house naked (though this would be a reasonably Swedish thing to do). But a level of bluntness helps. Naming things properly is a good place to start – whether that's your depression or your children's body parts – and practising letting go will go a long way, too. Mindfulness and box breathing (*see* pages 113–14) can help with the latter, and there's a lot to be said for facing your fears. Few things make you feel as invincible as walking into a situation that really scares you, and owning it. "Feel the fear and do it anyway," as author Susan Jeffers' self-help book of the same name proclaims.

## Attaining the *lagom* equilibrium

Last but not least, consider how you define happiness. Expectation is a powerful thing; if your aim is bubbling ecstasy, for example, life may seem disappointing a lot of the time. From a *lagom* perspective, sustainable happiness is just as much about acknowledging problems with a solutions-focused hat on and being present during the small moments of calm and bliss in your everyday life. Combine a blunt approach to language with a refusal to dramatize, and you'll be able to deal with all manner of feelings and experiences. No drama. Now, who wants to talk sex over coffee?

# A SWEDISH PSYCHOLOGIST ON LAGOM
## – why it works and what to do

**ERIKA STANLEY**

Erika is a psychologist based in Stockholm.

**BOX BREATHING**

Box breathing, or four-square breathing, is a technique used to tackle anxiety, either on demand as the symptoms appear or on a daily basis.

Simply get comfortable, then inhale and count to four. Hold your breath for another count to four, and release through your mouth, again on four. Wait four seconds before stopping or repeating.

The name "four-square breathing" comes from the idea of a four-sided visual guide to help you stay with your meditation.

**Cultural differences aside, your internal monologues and the way you deal with feelings and emotional experiences can very much be changed, regardless of where in the world you live. Here's a Swedish psychologist's take on a *lagom* approach to mental wellbeing.**

## Why *lagom*?

"Simply speaking, affect theory, which describes the organization of emotions and experienced feelings, suggests that we have a basic set of emotional states that are universal. These are meant to help us navigate through life – they're like a compass of sorts. So when we learn, depending on our experiences, either to suppress or to overreact to our own emotions, that compass doesn't work very well.

"We need to know how we feel about certain things in order to make sound decisions, yet without allowing the feelings to take over completely. Being in touch with your feelings in a *lagom* way is thought to be linked to good mental health and making sound decisions. That's the goal of many therapies, to find the right balance – to get better at identifying emotions you've perhaps learned to suppress and learn to manage and harbour feelings if you have a tendency to overreact.

## TOP TIP FOR PARENTS

There's a notion within attachment theory of "good enough", a concept quite similar to *lagom*. It implies that children will thrive and feel secure if they get a *lagom* amount of care from their parents. It's quite obvious why insufficient care is bad, but equally, too much can backfire.

It can be comforting for ambitious parents to know that you shouldn't strive to be a perfect person and parent, as your children then won't have a model for how to handle setbacks and adversities. There's also the risk that they'll spend their entire lives trying to live up to the same unattainable ideal as their parents, with poor self-esteem as a result. *Lagom* is best!

## TRY MINDFULNESS

Aiming for "non-judgmental awareness of the present moment", mindfulness helps you accept things you cannot change and has been proven beneficial in a great number of ways, including helping to prevent depression relapse. Through awareness and acceptance, mindfulness can help you trust in your experiences and encourage authentic living – including a full spectrum of experiences and emotions.

# An example to heed

"Think about burnout and exhaustion. This is a good example of when too much ambition and too much work – whether practical, mental or emotional – leads to poor mental health and mental illness. And that's no matter how positive or fun or exciting the work feels initially.

# How to find balance?

"There are endless techniques for centring yourself, like box breathing (*see* page 113), imagining that feelings are waves that come and go and so on. I personally tend to look to my future self when I'm worried and ask her whether she'll care about this particular thing. The answer is usually that she absolutely won't, which helps me put things into perspective.

# On acceptance and learning

"It can be useful to think in terms of a 'growth mindset' as opposed to a 'fixed mindset'. When things don't go as planned, take the opportunity to practise acceptance of failure. Reflect on what you've learned and try to take that with you to the next attempt, which will probably go much better."

# Socializing lagom:
## friends, clubs & neighbours

Swedes can be a reserved bunch at first, but with the help of all kinds of clubs and associations and a good dose of neighbourliness, they have managed to become an exceptionally trusting nation.

# SILENCE & BLUNTNESS
## – on functionalist language and honesty

## TALKING LAGOM

Culture and language are inextricably linked and, as such, experimentation with language is best done with caution. Yet there's a lot to be said for honesty and thinking before you speak. Over-polite precautions often just lead to confusion, misunderstandings and a waste of everyone's time. Find a diplomatic yet succinct way to say what you really mean, and people will respect you for it.

## LEARNING TO LISTEN

When practising your *lagom* talking, take a step back and get the benefit of learning to listen. Being a good listener can be a powerful thing; not only will your friends love you for it, but you'll become a better communicator, too.

Bump into a Swedish colleague with a quick "Hey, how are you?" and they'll stop to tell you in detail how they're honestly feeling and why. Swedes take language very literally, and this is a perfect example. Why ask how I am if you don't want the honest answer? They also mean what they say – and many of them are terrible liars. Remember that before asking what they think of that dress you've just bought.

Ever see those Facebook memes translating polite British expressions and everyday phrases to help visitors decipher the diplomatic, courteous language? There isn't one for Swedish, because you don't need one. Swedes will waste no time covering up what they're trying to say, nor will they expend it on superfluous words. Yes-or-no questions get yes-or-no answers – that's it. Call them blunt, but you can't criticize Swedes for wasting anyone's time.

There's a "what you see is what you get" approach to language in Sweden, which works quite well with the Law of Jante and people's aversion to talking too much about themselves (*see* page 11). But the silences are only awkward if you interpret them as such. Flip the coin and it's a guarantee that, when a Swede starts asking about you, you have their undivided and genuine attention.

# STAYING IN IS THE NEW GOING OUT

## – because it's comfortable, inexpensive and simply very *lagom*

What came first, the lack of bar culture or the tendency among Swedes to socialize in the home? You could ask the furniture and design giant IKEA, that proudly declared: "Home is the most important place in the world", or simply take both facts at face value and get on with learning how to socialize *lagom* style.

From *fika* (*see* page 40) playdates and birthday parties (*see* pages 68–9) to the notorious *förfest* – the phenomenon of holding a house party before a night out – and summer barbecues, Swedes are comparatively keen on inviting friends around. The get-together can be simple and laid back, with parents spontaneously swinging by their friends' house for a catch-up while feeding the kids macaroni and meatballs next to a pile of LEGO®. Conversely, they can be meticulously planned, including a pre-agreed potluck spread along with beers in front of the Eurovision Song Contest, complete with homemade Eurovision bingo and voting cards. All have a few very *lagom* things in common: the comfort of the home environment, the ease with which the gathering can be organized and the affordability of doing it yourself.

## Cooking up a recipe for success

A successful home get-together is about finding what unites you and your prospective guests. If you support the same football team, invite them over to watch the next match. If your shared interest is literature, suggest setting up a book club and invite readers over for coffee and book chats. But if you just want an excuse to show off your enviable cooking skills or your cute baby's cot, by all means throw a big party – just be wary of setting the bar too high if you want to be invited round to someone else's in return...

# JOIN A CLUB
## – on Swedish bonding

When Welshman Dylan Williams moved to Sweden for love, he was advised that in order to fit into Swedish society he had to join a club – so he joined Sweden's only male synchronized swimming team and made a movie-documentary – *Storyville: Sync or Swim* – about it.

Swedes love a group or association – anything for an organized get-together, ideally with a few rules. Popular movements have been important to Swedish society for a long time, most significantly since the 1800s when democratic rights were claimed. The temperance and workers' movements were significant from early on, and from around a century ago, popular education through associations and study groups has been a cornerstone of the Swedish democratic model. Today, study circles of three or more people can get public funding to meet and learn together.

**DID YOU KNOW?**

Sweden has the highest number of choirs per capita in the world, with about 600,000 Swedes regularly joining in on choral duties.

## Why joining a club is *lagom*

For most people, a regular group activity like a book club, a team sport or a campaigning group is very much about the social aspect. Not only does it help you to get out and do something you perhaps wouldn't or couldn't do on your own, but it also allows you to get to know like-minded people. In many ways, clubs celebrate some very *lagom* core values, notably an emphasis on the collective and an understanding that individual achievement doesn't always trump the enjoyment of a shared experience. Moreover, research shows that a group activity can help reduce stress and promote mental wellbeing by releasing the hormone oxytocin.

# LAGOM BUDDIES
## – on planning and a simple 360-degree friendship

Remember the concept of *förankringsprocessen* (*see* page 22)? I'm convinced that this semi-formal business process has an informal equivalent in the social and personal sphere. Of all the culture clashes, this is the one that drives my Irish husband up the wall the most: the constant planning.

**DID YOU KNOW?**
There's a strong sense of community in Sweden, and 92% of Swedes feel that they have someone they can rely on in time of need.

## The art of collective contentedness

To us Swedes, it's common sense – an unspoken rule. We ask each other when would be a good time to eat, what we should eat, where we should go and how we should get there. It's a guarantee of sorts: if everyone's opinion has been heard, no one can complain afterward; everyone can relax knowing that collective contentedness will ensue. Far from being awkward and complicated, this approach would be viewed by most as highly effective and congenial. When I think of my Swedish friendships, more than anything I think of them as incredibly uncomplicated. I know that, when we meet up, we'll all chip in – no one's being left behind.

## The wisdom of understatement

Swedes are often called reserved, and there's truth in that. But really get to know a Swede – invite them over to your home for *fika* (*see* page 40), join a club with them (*see* page 122) or meet them for a picnic with a game of *kubb* (*see* page 107) – and you'll see where the understated, *lagom* attitude pays off. It's a 360-degree relationship: they know your home, they find their way around your kitchen and they'll give you an honest opinion – completely without drama, every time.

# SWEDISH NEIGHBOURLINESS
## – on collective cleaning and communal laundry rooms

### Top tip #1

Throw a party on the green. Rope in your neighbours or put on a simple spread and invite them along. A more open relationship with your neighbours won't appear out of nowhere, but a chat and some food is a good place to start.

### Top tip #2

Create a pop-up neighbourhood book box. Write a sign and leave out a few books for people to borrow and return. Trust in action never looked better.

### Top tip #3

Ask for help with watering of flowers and then offer to help in return. Many people these days find it harder to ask for help than to offer a helping hand, so by opening that door to your neighbour, you increase the likelihood of them asking you when they need something.

With a society built on trust and a notion of shared responsibility, it'll come as no surprise that many Swedish apartment blocks are owned and run by cooperative housing associations, which look after everything from property tax and major renovation works to maintenance of the shared laundry rooms. Purchase a flat as part of one of these co-ops, and you'll buy yourself some of that shared responsibility – including the obligation to take part in what is known to most Swedes as the big, annual spring clean.

Don't fret – the big cleaning day is not as dull as it sounds. Flower beds may need to be refreshed and hedges trimmed, but you may also find yourself talking about football with a new neighbour with coffee in one hand and the secateurs in the other. If the bonding goes well, you might even end up in another neighbour's kitchen for a nightcap before you call it a day.

## Acting on trust

From booking laundry slots a week in advance to covering the bill for shared garbage collection, it all comes down to trust. In most global happiness rankings, people who consider themselves to be happy also report a high level of trust in fellow citizens as well as elected representatives. Trust thy neighbour to contribute during the big spring clean and to leave the laundry room nice and tidy, and you'll be that bit happier. After all, who doesn't want a good, trustworthy neighbour? Yes, you guessed it: research agrees that good relationships with neighbours make us happier.

# THE MOST LAGOM OF HOLIDAYS
## – come rain or shine, get a caravan

**I remember laughing at the idea of caravan holidays. Then I had kids. Maybe it's the thought of being able to throw everything into a caravan, close the door and drive off that sounds so liberating, or perhaps I've just become more Swedish with age. A caravan holiday, or a *husvagnssemester*, is as *lagom* as vacations get.**

## Simple pleasures

Cutting out air miles as you set off on country roads while others jet off to Thailand immediately ticks the eco box. Then you arrive at your chosen camping location, also known as Swedish holiday utopia. The Swedish version has a lake for swimming whenever you please, an old kiosk for buying ice cream and the all-important *lördagsgodis* (*see* page 64), a mini golf course and maybe a playground for some entertainment, alongside communal shower and toilet facilities. Wherever you go, the secret is in the complete lack of extravagance.

## Back to nature

If a trip to Bali is the Porsche of holidays, a caravan vacation is the Volvo. It's not fancy or luxurious, and it's far from pretentious, but if what you want from your summer break is communion with nature, doing nothing other than swimming, chilling and spending time with your family, it might be all you've ever dreamed of.

Worried about unwelcome geniality and shared showers? Don't be – a picturesque cottage on a lonely island in the archipelago or a beach hut in your nearest seaside town tick the *lagom* box, too.

# Lagom for the planet:
## the environment & sustainable living

With an eco glossary and some tips from an eco-warrior, take the first steps toward becoming a more conscious consumer and reap the benefits of a more lightweight attitude to material possessions.

6

# THINKING LAGOM, GOING GREEN
## – on environmental awareness as part of the Swedish consciousness

### SWEDISH ECO FACTS

• Only 1% of all household waste in Sweden ends up in landfill – the rest is recycled or used to produce heat, electricity or vehicle fuel.

• Renewable energy sources account for 52% of the energy production, of which almost 95% comes from hydropower.

• Stockholm was the European Union's first ever European Green Capital.

• 90% of all aluminium cans in Sweden are recycled.

### MAKE RECYCLING EASY

In line with the *lagom* ethos, recycling shouldn't be hard. Invest in a good wastebin system that works for you, and soon the sorting will become second nature.

I must have been about ten when we learned about ozone layer depletion in school. I still remember the drawing on the blackboard: the rounded layer protecting the Earth, the UV rays bouncing off it and the rays that made it through. We were told about ice melt in Arctic and the polar bears that would soon be extinct. The enemy was the aerosol spray; suddenly, otherwise intensely vain school girls stopped bringing hairspray for the post-PE shower, because who wants to be responsible for killing polar bears anyway?

## Adopting the recycling habit

We must have learned about recycling, too, but this somehow made less of an impact on me. It wasn't on the front pages, nor was the link to the extinction of nice, innocent animals explicitly made. Yet slowly but surely it was becoming a natural part of everyday life in Sweden. Separate waste paper bins appeared everywhere, and the average Swede started learning about composting. A legislated deposit paid on glass bottles and aluminium cans to incentivize recycling was already deeply ingrained in our consciousness and habits. People bought glass-bottled fizzy drinks by the crate, only to return each bottle to the crate after drinking, then turn up at the supermarket with a crateful of bottles to recycle – a very tangible example of recycling as habitual reality, when you think about it.

## Committing to the eco cause

I was a good bit older when a group of activists set up a campaign against the supposedly extortionate cost of travelling by public transport in Stockholm, encouraging people to illegally travel for free in protest. I thought they were on to something – until I heard the counter-argument that maybe it wasn't the brightest idea ever to abuse a system you fundamentally believe in, evading the statistics of how many people actually do.

That argument speaks volumes about the attitude in Sweden to toeing the line generally and using public transport specifically. There are plenty of exceptions to confirm the rule, but I have rarely seen public transport commuters as willing and contented at 8am on a Monday morning as Swedes in Stockholm. There's an understanding and consensus to hold it all together. Everyone knows they're in this together; everyone knows that public transport is part and parcel of a greener world.

## Back to the issue of trust

Swedes are generally far more trusting than other nations, and it shows – why bother with laborious recycling and composting if you don't trust that your neighbour will follow suit? Ideas about avoiding plastic wrappers and opting for organic alternatives are taking root because there is less cynicism than elsewhere. It has become an unspoken agreement – perhaps not in all corners of society, but certainly in the mainstream – that this is how we must live, that as a concerted effort it really is worth it.

# ECO GLOSSARY
## – Swedish terms for a *lagom* eco lifestyle

Finding that *lagom* balance in your consumption habits is all about a shift in your mindset. These terms go some way toward describing the habits and systems that have helped Swedes make that shift – some of which might inspire you on your quest for a more symbiotic, *lagom* relationship with the environment.

### Köpstopp

Committing to *köpstopp* means deciding not to buy anything at all for a given period of time. It's an acknowledgement that, a lot of the time, we don't actually need the things we buy. Some people opt for a month of no purchases other than food. Besides saving you money and being kind to the environment, it often brings a sense of freedom from the modern-day consumer lifestyle. Some would even call it addictive...

**DID YOU KNOW?**

Turning your thermostat down by just one degree could reduce your heating bills by about 10%.

LED bulbs don't just use roughly 90% less energy than the average incandescent bulb – they also last around 20 times longer.

### Plastbanta

The Institute of Language and Folklore's 2014 list of new Swedish words welcomed this eco-warrior, loosely translating as "plastic detox". As such, it's quite self-explanatory and a habit that can be built into your everyday life little by little, wherever you live. Think before you buy: is there a non-plastic alternative to the product you've picked? Plastic children's toys are known to contain a great deal of toxins and chemicals. Opt for wood, bamboo or stainless steel wherever possible, and your home and health will thank you for it.

"Shops are starting
to pop up where you
can buy everything
by weight."

Shops are starting to pop up where you can buy everything from food to clothes by weight. Just bring your own jars, tins and bags, and you are good to go! For inspiration, check out Gram Malmö, Sweden's first packaging-free grocery store.

## Panta

If you've ever been to a Swedish supermarket, you will have seen the queues of Swedes with their bags and crates full of empty cans and bottles, ready for the recycling machines. *Pant,* which is clearly labelled on aluminium cans and plastic bottles at the time of purchase, is a legislated deposit in the form of a small amount of money paid as part of the product price and returned upon recycling of the can or bottle. Now, if you're familiar with the fact that Swedes tend to bring their own drink to house parties (this is what the *förfest* is all about – *see* page 121), you'll begin to understand why poor students are very happy hosts.

## Oumph!

*Oumph*! is just one – albeit a hugely popular one – of the many vegetarian and vegan alternatives to meat that have appeared in Swedish supermarkets in recent years, with an estimated 10% of Swedes following a vegetarian diet and a third of the population expressing a wish to avoid meat to a greater extent than they already do. Södra Teatern, one of Stockholm's trendy bars, recently introduced an all-vegetarian menu, where guests have to opt in to get meat on their plate rather than opting out to avoid it, and many supermarkets are actively working to encourage consumers to eat less meat. With more and more eco-warriors arguing that the meat industry is one of the world's greatest environmental hazards, why not make your "meat-free Monday" a "meaty Monday" instead, going veggie or even vegan the rest of the week?

# TESTIMONY OF A SWEDISH ECO-WARRIOR
## – on going green, more sustainable habits and adding soul to your home

**ANGELIQA CRAMNELL**

Angeliqa, 28, is studying behavioural science. She is married to Tobias, 32, a construction engineer. They live in a 1930s house in a town in central Sweden with their daughters Miranda, 5 and Judith, 2.

Living green on a budget and having a nice, cosy home with a family of four – it can't be possible? With a *lagom* lifestyle of conscious consumption, responsible recycling and eco awareness, it is.

## On becoming an eco-warrior

"I saw a documentary when I was 12 about the meat industry and how the animals were treated, and it made a strong impression on me. I became a vegetarian that same day and have been for 16 years now. Tobias and the children aren't vegetarians, but they eat veggie food with me most days.

"I became a vegetarian for ethical reasons but quickly realized that there are other, equally important reasons for choosing a greener life. What started with meat quickly escalated to an awareness of how our way of life in the Western world has significant impact globally.

"Our strategies for green living became all the more important when Miranda was born. I started reading up about everything; the environmental impact of plastic toys led to a decision to go on a plastic detox – *plastbanta* – and buy nothing but eco toys made of wood. We made our own porridge and bought organic flannels, and eventually we bought an old house with a large garden that enabled us to grow our own food. We now grow different kinds of berries, fruits and vegetables. The kids love it and join in with everything from planting to harvesting.

### #1: Use and tweak what you have

A lot of the time, I think we buy new things even if we don't have to. There are so many items in our homes that can be used for other purposes: cans make great planting pots and lanterns; old boxes can be turned into planters, storage boxes or a toy home for dinosaurs.

### #2: Buy second hand

When something must be bought, look in second-hand shops first. Not everything is cheaper to buy second hand, but it's significantly better for the environment and often really attractive. When I buy a second-hand lamp, I know that it's had a life before me and I enjoy thinking about what conversations have taken place underneath it. It adds soul to the home.

## On IKEA's sustainability initiative

"When a friend told me about IKEA's "hållbara ihop", or "sustainable together", a project aiming to raise awareness among consumers about a sustainable lifestyle, I applied to see if IKEA could help us become even more conscious in the way we live.

"The participants went through various steps to reduce their carbon footprint, such as changing to LED bulbs and reducing food waste and water consumption. We had done most of it already but tried to push ourselves to improve, and among other things we got even better at reducing our food waste. We also optimized our recycling together with IKEA and got an entire new recycling system in our basement.

## On *köpstopp* – a purchase cap

"I realized last winter that we'd increased our consumption of newly produced products like toys and clothes. It's hard for us to cut down on clothes, as our children are in an eco kindergarten with an outdoor profile, so their outerwear is worn out quickly and needs to be replaced – but we had to do something.

"We decided to go for full *köpstopp* – so buying absolutely nothing – with regard to everything bar outerwear for the children whenever it had to be replaced, and to do it for at least three months. It's been much easier than we thought it would be, and even if we'll lift the cap at some stage, our consumption habits have improved massively."

# THINK BEFORE YOU BUY
## – top tips for more sustainable consumer habits

**Frustrated by inadequate recycling facilities and public transport where you live? Don't fret. Reviewing what you buy and how you do it is a great place to start and can make a huge difference in reducing your carbon footprint.**

### PLASTIC? NO THANKS

You might not be ready to ditch every plastic item in your home, but why buy more? Look for bamboo, wood or metal alternatives, and check food packaging – some things have layers of the stuff.

### BUY PRE-LOVED

Second-hand shops are full of bargains in great condition and with stories to tell. They will often do your finances a favour, too – but even when they don't, you can be sure that your conscience will thank you, as your carbon footprint is minimized.

### LEAVE THE CAR AT HOME

Not everyone can live without a car, but most of us can manage without during the weekly shop. If you can't cycle and throw the bags in a bike trolley, find out who delivers to your door. Most supermarkets offer online shopping, allowing you to plan ahead – and the small charge is often a fraction of what the petrol, parking and impulse purchases would add up to.

### COUNT TO TEN

The *"Räkna till 10"* or *"Count to 10"* campaign is encouraging Swedes to try the count-to-10 method: when you're about to buy something new/throw something out, count to 10 and ask yourself if you really need it/if it can be fixed, and then decide. Try it!

## AVOID BULK BUYING

Stocking up on buy-one-get-one-free items? Research shows that those who bulk buy also waste more. Bulk buying is often a good intention without a realistic plan, and it's a problem worth treating; roughly one-third of all food produced for human consumption globally goes to waste. So buy *lagom* – sufficient, but not too much – and then shop again when you truly need more.

# FREEDOM & FLEXIBILITY
## – the benefits of a lightweight attitude to material possessions

### THREE BENEFITS OF A LIGHTWEIGHT LIFESTYLE

**#1.** It's habitual, almost like a reprogramming of the brain to rid it of the patterns formed by consumer society. Much like you're probably more likely to crave carrots than cake after a run, a good decluttering session will make shopping seem less appealing.

**#2.** You'll have more space when all that stuff is gone, which subsequently saves you time as you'll find what you're looking for more easily – and cleaning will be a breeze. Moreover, a peaceful space contributes to a peaceful mind, so you might experience a boost in creativity.

**#3.** Most people keen on elimination and minimalism swear by the mind's tendency to focus more on experiences than material possessions once the majority of the clutter is gone. To many people, this mindfulness provides a potent sense of freedom – one no money can buy.

A conscious, *lagom* approach to consumption is good not just for the environment but for our bank balances, too. But there's another level to the non-material ways, linked to a freedom from the pressures of consumer society, and it has sparked an entire movement of "sell everything" enthusiasts who get rid of their possessions, leave their homes and hit the road in search for adventure, freedom and inner peace.

Slightly less extreme but just as keen on scaling down are the minimalists, heralding an elimination method. These people often own nothing more than what can fit in a backpack, "just enough" possessions, including a very basic wardrobe as well as whatever hygienic products and digital gadgets they need. A minimalist experiment went viral on Facebook recently, encouraging people to challenge their friends to a month of arithmetically progressive cleansing, getting rid of one item on day one, two on day two and so on until a total of 469 things had been chucked.

# Lagom for life:
## an honest approach to happiness

Sweden is changing, and so is *lagom*.
Here's how to take it with you –
and why I think you should.

7

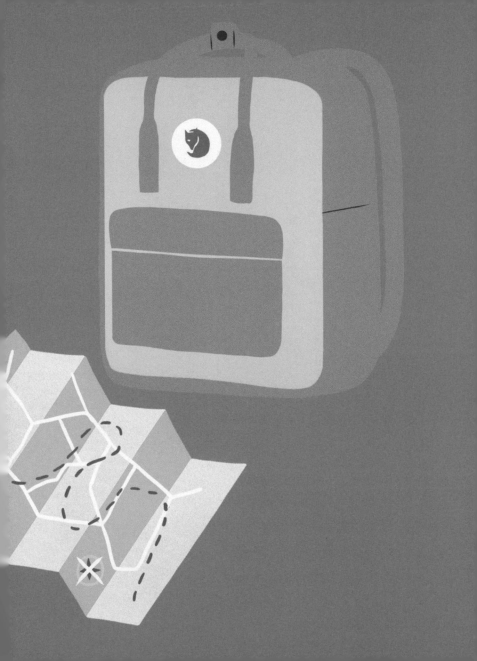

# A CHANGING SWEDEN

## – on me as a *lagom* advocate and allowing *lagom* to raise its game

When I first told my Swedish friends that I was writing this book, some of them were confused. "Are we really that happy?" they asked. My answer is that yes, to a great extent we are – but it's a *lagom* kind of happiness.

What's funny about Swedes questioning whether we as a nation are really all that happy is that pretty much every single one of them would be of the "look at how we do it in Sweden" school of thought, if less or more explicitly. The idea that we're doing something right, that Swedish society with all of its systems and values is good and beneficial, few will argue with. In fact, we all agree that it contributes to a good life.

This book has looked, among other things, at work–life balance, the Swedish relationship to food and exercise, environmentally conscious living and the case for a *lagom* approach to feelings. The takeaway, if you ask me, is that happiness in a sustainable sense is not about extremes. Not in the sense of elation and hysterical laughter, even if those can be good, too; not in terms of bigger houses and more money and rigid fitness regimes. It's about how we join the dots, how we make necessary evils less evil and meaningful moments last.

"Happiness in a
sustainable sense is
not about extremes."

## *Lagom* as a force for good

Friends of mine who didn't initially question Swedish happiness levels had another concern. They looked at me, smiled and said: "You? Really?" Of course, taking on writing a book on top of a full-time job as a mother of two who so happened to also be in the middle of buying a house, was not exactly a sign that I've got my work–life balance all figured out. What can I say? I'm still learning.

But remember this: Sweden is not what it was when the Law of Jante was first coined (*see* page 11), nor is it now what it was when I grew up. It's full of people from all corners of the globe, bursting with new impressions and continuously working to embrace all kinds of cultures and flavours that are far from traditionally *lagom*. It's an outward-looking, modern, multicultural country, and it's all the better for it.

This book is full of extreme generalizations, as any book describing a specific culture must be. But it's also taking all that is good about *lagom* and turning its back on everything the concept has been criticized for: its suffocating norms and dislike of boldness. It's looking at the ways the concept of *lagom* has shaped the Swedish way of life and contributed to its quirks and secrets, allowing you to pick 'n' mix in whatever way it suits you. I know that's what I'm doing – trying a *lagom* approach to *lagom*.

Right now, when the ethos is being heralded as a route to happiness, when the country of semi-skimmed milk is full of those who view the cow as holy and those who opt for oat milk or no milk at all, *lagom* can't be a one-way street but is allowed to raise its game. If *lagom* is about striving toward becoming a more conscious consumer, looking after your neighbour as well as your fellow citizen and creating the space, literally and figuratively, to be able to contain all kinds of emotions and experiences, then surely it can only be a force for good?

# FROM HERE TO LAGOM
## – tasks and thoughts to take with you

A force for good and looking after your fellow citizen? Well that's just corny and sentimental, says the ever-blunt Swede, refusing to mince words. If you're still stuck for inspiration and sceptical of the corny talk, follow these steps to see if a Swedish-style *lagom* approach to life is for you.

### #1: Invite some friends around for *fika* (*see* page 40)

You don't have to bake your own buns, but see what happens when you remove the atmosphere of the bar and the distractions of consumer culture and sit down face to face with a coffee and a few candles.

### #2: Have a wardrobe clear out (*see* page 85)

Be bold. If you haven't worn it in six months, task yourself with wearing it in the next week, or pass it on – and don't replace it.

### #3: Count to 10

The next time you need to go shopping, put your critical hat on and try the count-to-10 method (*see* page 144). I bet you'll start enjoying putting things back on the shelves and walking away.

### #4: Declutter your home

It doesn't have to be major. Fix a cable that's been annoying you or sort through your children's toys to give away ones they've outgrown.

### #5: Try a new outdoor activity

Find the most *lagom* outdoor activity you can think of, and give it a go (*see* page 106). Go foraging (*see* page 54), enjoy a swim in a lake or build a snow castle. Worst case: it's not for you but you've breathed in some fresh air. Best case: you'll make a habit out of prioritizing downtime in nature.

### #6: Offer to help a neighbour

Maybe they need their plants watered or their dog walked. Maybe they don't need anything – in which case a tray of freshly-baked cinnamon buns will be a lovely surprise.

### #7: Leave work on time

Decide that you're leaving work on the dot tomorrow, no matter what happens – and honour it. What's the worst that could happen?

### #8: Enjoy your first *fredagsmys*

Rope in family or a friend, and spend a Friday evening perfecting the art of vegging (*see* page 24). It's an addictive ritual – trust me.

## "You give and you take"

As someone who left Sweden sneering at *lagom*, I was fascinated by what author Jonas Gardell said when I interviewed him in 2016. "*Lagom* should be Sweden's great export to the world," he said. "In failing to market it properly, we've failed to market our greatest strength." To think that a gay man who's written extensively about love and loneliness, who has given guest sermons in a Stockholm church and once wrote about God as "a black, lesbian woman", who has an opinion on pretty much everything and is never slow to share it – to think that he would view *lagom* as Sweden's greatest strength was revolutionary to me.

"You give and you take; that's what should be the great Swedish export to the world, to all ideologies and religions," he said. "Truth doesn't have to be black or white, but with *lagom* we can avoid extremism. See, a lot fits within the parameters for *lagom*. I'm quite an oddball, and even I fit in. But the benefit of *mellanmjölk* [semi-skimmed milk] is that we don't have to kill each other – we can accept compromise."

Gardell can be himself and adored for it, not in spite of but very much thanks to a progressive country that doesn't shut down debate out of exhaustion and awkwardness and instead keeps on going until consensus is reached. If there's one thing I really love about my home country, that's it: this insistence on doing things right, on making an effort when needed, be it for ourselves or for the common good.

And then, we *fika*.

(page numbers in *italic* type refer
to photographs and captions)

## Resources

**Page 29** Swedish parents' entitlement to parental leave: www.sweden.se/society/10-things-that-make-sweden-family-friendly/

**Page 30** "What does equality have to do with lagom?" www.ted.com/talks/michael_kimmel_why_gender_equality_is_good_for_everyone_men_included/transcript?language=en

**Page 30** 2016 Happiness Index: www.foxbusiness.com/features/2017/01/30/when-it-comes-to-employee-happiness-worklifebalance-offers-best-roi.html

## Picture Credits

**Angeliqa Cramnell** 68, 141, 142. **Anna Lidström/@anotherblog.se** 2, 83, 84. **Even Steven Agenturer** 91. **String® (www.string.se)** 88. **Alamy Stock Photo** Andreas von Einsiedel 75; Apeloga/Astrakan Images 95; David Schreiner/Folio Images 57; HERA FOOD 43; tf2/picturesbyrob 61; Vipula Samarakoon 66. **Getty Images** Johan Mrd/Folio 76; Johner Images 27; Jonathan Nackstrand/AFP 134; Maskot 21; Romona Robbins Photography 128. **Imagebank.sweden.se** Amanda Westerbom 80; Faramarz Gosheh 155; Fredrik Broman 15; Henrik Trygg 103; Johan Willner 111; Jonas Overödder 53; Sara Ingman 99; Susanne Walström 28; Tove Freiij 41. **istockphoto.com** Frank and Helena 152. **Shutterstock** Alliance 33; FabrikaSimf 71; Magdanatka 51; oneinchpunch 104; Pressmaster 115; Rawpixel.com 44, 156–157; Rido 124.

## Thank You

To all the *lagom* Swedes featured in this book, for your time, opinions and generosity.

To www.sweden.se, for perfectly user-friendly, fascinating and inspiring information.

And to Team Dunne, for giving me the space, the support and the love to write this book.